ECONOMIC NATIONALISM
IN OLD AND NEW STATES

By Professor Harry G. Johnson
ECONOMIC POLICIES TOWARDS LESS DEVELOPED COUNTRIES
ESSAYS IN MONETARY ECONOMICS
INTERNATIONAL TRADE AND ECONOMIC GROWTH
MONEY, TRADE AND ECONOMIC GROWTH

ECONOMIC NATIONALISM
IN
OLD AND NEW STATES

edited and with chapters by

HARRY G. JOHNSON

A publication of
The Committee for the Comparative Study of New Nations
University of Chicago

LONDON: GEORGE ALLEN AND UNWIN LTD

C

247979

Econs.

PRINTED IN GREAT BRITAIN
BY UNWIN BROTHERS LIMITED
WOKING AND LONDON

INTRODUCTION

Harry G. Johnson

The Committee for the Comparative Study of New Nations of the University of Chicago is composed of social scientists who have found it useful to meet together regularly to discuss their research problems, approaches, and findings. Members, working individually with the tools of their separate disciplines on some particular aspect of the problems posed by the new nations, together seek to derive insights from the comparison of country findings and of the methods and results of the different social sciences. To this end, the Committee each year organizes a seminar, under the chairmanship of one of its members, with a central theme derived by consensus from its past deliberations and findings and its perception of new areas for joint exploration.

By 1964, the Committee had formed the view: first, that the comparative approach needed to be extended beyond the study of the new nations themselves to include study of the formative historical experiences of the now established states if it were to yield its full fruitfulness; and second, that its earliest discussions of the problems of economic development, with which all the new nations are in one way or another concerned, indicated a need for exploration of development policy and planning and particularly of the nature and influence of economic nationalism which seemed to be responsible for many of the difficulties that the new nations have encountered. Accordingly, the theme of economic nationalism was selected for the 1964–65 seminar, under my chairmanship. In accordance with our recognition of the need for a broader comparative approach, the seminar program focused on the question of economic nationalism in general rather than on economic nationalism as manifested in new states. Additional time was devoted to the exploration of what could be learned from the experience of nationalism in nineteenth-century Europe and in contemporary countries not appropriately describable as new nations. Throughout the year, however, our concern was with the relevance of this experience to the new nations that are our common interest. A common basis for discussion was established by the introductory paper of the series, which attempted to establish a conceptual framework and to pose the key questions suggested by our earlier work on the problem of economic development.

The papers collected in this volume are those of the seminar papers which in the Committee's judgment seemed worth putting on more permanent record for others concerned with the study of new nations and which, at the same time, formed a connected unity in which the interplay of the different social science disciplines and of specialized knowledge of different nations, new and old, that occurs in the Committee can be seen at work. These papers are presented to our colleagues as working papers intended to carry forward the discussion, not as final works of scholarship. Not all the papers which contributed to the development of our ideas are included: some are instead being incorporated in monographic studies by their authors. On the other hand, one paper in this volume was published shortly before the 1964-65 seminar but reflects in part ideas derived from the Committee's earlier work; another originated after the seminar sessions ended (as a lecture in the Committee's annual graduate course, "An Introduction to the Study of New States") that attempts to place some of the thinking of the seminar in the broader context of the ideology of economic policy in the new nations.

The first paper in this volume presents a formal theory of nationalism that attempts to relate the phenomenon to a rational theory of government processes and to explain the consequences of economic nationalism in terms of the exchange by the community of real private consumption for collective consumption of a "public good," national ownership and control of the economic system. This analysis suggests two possible roles for economic nationalism in the establishment of a new state. One is that nationalism is a necessary basis for effecting the social transformation required to establish a modern state capable of the take-off into self-sustaining growth. Manning Nash's case study of Mexico argues that this has been the role of nationalism and the national revolution in that country; but he points to certain unique features of Mexican experience — notably the pragmatism of government intervention in and control over the development process, and the fact that land reform has been used to pacify the peasantry while the modernization of agriculture has been effected in new regions of the country — which make that experience unreliable as a guide to likely developments in the contemporary new nations. The other possibility is that collective consumption of the public good of nationalism is the only way in which a new nation can hope to raise its real income, given adverse initial economic and social circumstances; nationalism would thus serve as a substitute for the modernization process. Aristide Zolberg's case study of the rapid transformation of Malian economic policy from a rational and sensible internationalist approach well grounded in Marxist theory into financially unsustainable nationalistic extremism leads him to conclude that Mali exemplifies this alternative. It may be, however, that our perspective on Malian experience — as on the phenomenon of nationalistic extremism in the new nations in general — is too short, and that a succession of nationalistic experimentations is necessary to lay the basis for social modernization. Certainly the 1966 wave of depositions of one-party leaders in new states suggests that the phase of extreme nationalism is unstable; but in this, as in other social contexts, change is not necessarily identifiable with progress.

Arcadius Kahan's paper explores the European experience of nineteenth-century nationalism, focusing on the political question of whether nationalism and a concern for economic development went together and on the economic question of whether nationalistic economic policies actually promoted development. On the first question he produces evidence to the contrary, and suggests that the industrial requirements of an advancing military technology, rather than a nationalistic concern for the promotion of economic development as such, gave rise to the emphasis on industrialization policy as the means of creating a modern state. This suggestion evokes the intriguing thought, related to my own concluding contribution to this volume, that the ideology of economic policy in the new states relies to an important extent on stereotypes inherited from the nineteenth-century struggle for power in Europe, which stereotypes are far removed from the objective reality confronting the new nations of the twentieth century. On the second question — whether nationalistic economic policies really helped much to promote economic development in the European countries he considers — Kahan arrives at a predominantly negative conclusion. While this conclusion rests more on broad historical judgment than on firm quantitative evidence, it is a judgment, I believe, with which most economic historians and international trade experts would agree. However, the em-

pirical results follow almost inevitably from the nature of nineteenth-century nationalism as Kahan describes it, and it remains
to be investigated whether twentieth-century nationalistic development planning has made a more positive contribution than
nineteenth-century protectionism to the economic growth of the
countries practicing it.

Nineteenth-century European nationalism and nation-building
were in large part a response to the industrial preeminence of
Great Britain. The question naturally arises of how far, if at all,
British economic policy was influenced by nationalism or — its
corollary for a successful country — imperialism. Roger Weiss
examines this question in the third paper in this volume. He concludes that the free-trade prescriptions of Adam Smith were
nationalistic, in the sense of being concerned with the welfare of
Britain rather than of the world, but that this raised no real conflicts of principle between nationalistic (in this sense) and cosmopolitan policies. He also argues that, whether British economic
nationalism is conceived in the broad sense as a concern to maximize the economic welfare of the British nation as a whole, or in
the narrower sense of a concern of a particular group — the manufacturing class — to maximize their own welfare by using their
power within the British political system, nationalism was an
extremely weak and ineffective force in those areas of policy in
which it might have been expected to operate.

The problem of what nationalism in economic policy really
means is raised by Robert Dernberger in the fourth paper presented here. Dernberger, an expert on contemporary Communist
China, contrasts nationalism with the internationalist philosophy
of Communism and argues that — at least in the Chinese context
he describes — Communism is a more powerful force than nationalism in commanding support for a revolution, but a less powerful
force for mobilizing the community in support of the process of
modernization. He attributes the increasing resort of the Chinese
Communist regime to nationalism as a mobilizing force to the
pressures of expedience rather than interpreting it as clear evidence of doctrinal inconsistency. The question of how to identify
nationalistic policy under a Communist regime raises some difficult conceptual problems which we were forced to recognize in
the Committee's discussions but which we have been unable to
resolve in any useful fashion. It is worthwhile to point out, how-

ever, that Zolberg's paper on Mali evidences the same phenomenon as Dernberger describes, but in a much starker form. The Union Soudanaise moved from an analytical Marxist philosophical orientation on Mali's economic development problems to a rabidly nationalistic one in a very brief span of time, and in so doing has provided support for Dernberger's thesis about the relative superiority of nationalism over Communism as a tool of social mobilization and the generation of consensus.

Manning Nash's case study of Mexico is designed in part as a test of whether nationalism is a means of sidestepping the hard issues of social transformation and modernization that merely wastes time and resources, or a necessary cost of or investment in that process — an input into modernization, as he calls it. Nash argues strongly and persuasively for the latter interpretation of the Mexican case. His analysis appears in sharp conflict with Kahan's findings on the role of nationalism in the economic development of Europe in the nineteenth century; but the two papers can readily be reconciled by reference to the historical evolution of the phenomenon of nationalism itself. Nash concludes his paper by questioning the usefulness of general models of nationalism in understanding particular cases. Such questioning of our basic assumption that the new nations in some sense constitute a universe of observation capable of yielding valid generalizations is both necessary and salutary. However, it is precisely case studies such as Nash has provided that delineate the scope for and limitations of theoretical generalizations.

Apart from its relevance in the context of the study of new nations, Nash's study of the Mexican case should be of particular interest to American social scientists, since Mexico, though it borders on the United States, is virtually a terra incognita in terms of scholarly research into and analysis of its economic, political, and social problems by Americans, and especially in terms of public awareness in the United States of the character of these problems. My own paper on economic nationalism in Canadian policy has, I hope, a similar general interest. In it I have attempted something which I believe is unusual for a contemporary economist: to trace to their sources in the thinking of particular influential individuals the ideas about the working of the economic system and about economic policy that dominate popular discussion of economic policy problems and governmental

policy itself. I have also attempted to show how in certain cases
the implementation of the ideas in policy decisions has had economic consequences that have "fed back" as evidence apparently
validating the original ideas.

In this respect, my paper is a companion piece to Aristide Zolberg's. Zolberg analyzes the process by which a government that
initially displayed an understanding of the problems of economic
development confronting it superior to that of the governments
of surrounding countries retrogressed rapidly into nationalistic
extremism once it had become responsible for the formulation and
execution of policy. He demonstrates in particular the inevitable
self-reinforcing quality of the resort to increasingly nationalistic
policies and the ultimate futility of this line of evolution. Both
the Malian and the Canadian cases indicate, in their widely different ways, how easy it is for the political process to lose contact
with objective economic reality in the formulation of development
policy, and suggest that when this happens increasing nationalism
serves as a substitute in consumption for the rising level of living
standards that the politicians are incapable of delivering so rapidly
as promised.

The final chapter of the book presents an effort to sort out and
assess the influence and implications of three tightly interwoven
strands in the inheritance of ideas regarding the contemporary
development problem: political and economic nationalism, economic theories about the development problem, and the political
attitudes of developed and less developed countries toward one
another. In a sense, it represents a personal concluding chapter
to several years of work within the Committee for the Comparative Study of New Nations, of which only the latest aspect is
recorded in the preceding chapters.

The papers included in this volume are, as previously stated,
presented as work in progress rather than as final products of
scholarship. In retrospect, as various writers have indicated, several subjects appear to offer inviting opportunities for further
theoretical and empirical research. Kahan, Dernberger, and Weiss
all indicate that the concept of economic nationalism requires
both a historical taxonomy and considerable theoretical refine-
ment if it is to be made a reliable operational concept for the
analysis of economic policy. Their work and my own suggest that
a comparative study of the inheritance of nationalistic ideas by

the new nations from their European colonial masters might be extremely illuminating. Nash points to the need for comparative study to ascertain the conditions under which nationalism can serve as an input into the modernization process — an "investment in human capital" with a long-run payoff — and the alternative conditions under which nationalism blocks modernization and the creation of a viable state. Zolberg's paper suggests the desirability of a comparative study of the political dynamics of the assumption of power by a government that is committed to promoting economic development in a new nation which lacks the human and material resources to mount a development program capable of accomplishing it. Other topics worthy of further study will no doubt occur to the reader of this volume.

I cannot conclude this Introduction without recording my heart-felt thanks to Estelle Stinespring, Secretary of the Committee for the Comparative Study of New Nations, for her invaluable services not only in performing the technical task of seeing this volume through the press, but also in assuming a substantial share of the responsibility for the intellectual task of ensuring that the ideas of the contributors be expressed as clearly and unambiguously as possible.

CONTENTS

1. A THEORETICAL MODEL OF ECONOMIC NATIONALISM IN NEW AND DEVELOPING STATES

Harry G. Johnson

Nationalism in new and developing states is a complex problem of increasing concern to both political scientists and economists. To the political scientist, nationalism appears on the one hand as an integrative ideological force facilitating the establishment of a viable and cohesive nation-state; on the other hand, ethnic groupings, especially when they coincide with geographical, linguistic, and religious differences, generate the phenomenon of nationalism within the state and constitute a threat to the political stability of the state and the prospects for its survival. In addition, nationalism is a factor fundamental to the understanding of the ideological role of the concepts of colonialism and imperialism in the political life of formerly colonial states. Equally, to the economist, nationalism appears on the one hand as a driving force responsible for the urge of less developed countries (of which the majority are new states) to accelerate their economic development by economic planning, and on the other hand as the major political influence responsible for the fact that many features of the policies, concepts, and methods of economic development planning in such countries either do not make economic sense or would make economic sense only in certain specific and rather exceptional economic circumstances the actual presence of which no one has felt it necessary to establish by empirical economic research.

This last point may be illustrated by a variety of examples. In the first place, both public pronouncements in developing countries and the literature on economic development are pervaded by an emphasis on industrialization as the necessary path to economic development, despite the fact that many economists, looking either to past economic history or to the current situation in the less developed countries, have concluded that the development of agriculture or of exports of certain natural resource products constitutes their logical path to economic development. Second, concerning the choice of industries to be fostered by development

Reprinted with permission from the *Political Science Quarterly*, LXXX (June, 1965), 169–85.

policy, there is a marked tendency to consider certain industries as strategic, almost regardless of the size of the country, its location, or its available skills. Which industries these are depends in large part on the stage of development. In the earliest stages of development, a steel industry is generally regarded as the sine qua non of economic development, even though steel requires a massive investment of capital and the world steel industry has tended to suffer from chronic over-capacity rather than excessive pressure of demand. In more advanced countries, like Canada, Australia, the Union of South Africa, Mexico, and Argentina, the sine qua non of development is a domestic automotive industry, even though the establishment of such an industry involves essentially the local production of American or European models at costs substantially above the prices of imports. In countries that are generally regarded as advanced, other than the United States, a comparable emphasis has been placed on the production of atomic energy, even though the commercial profitability of that form of power is not yet firmly established. As indicated, an economic justification for regarding the specific industrial activities mentioned as strategic is difficult to provide; instead, the selection of what activity is strategic seems to be governed by rivalry with and imitation of other nations that are considered in some sense to be superior.

A third example, different in nature, is the almost universal prevalence of a preference for public enterprise over private enterprise. Such a preference is not necessarily a question of nationalism — it may be a consequence of political philosophy — but it frequently seems to be dictated by nationalism rather than by socialist political principle. The problem for the economist here is to explain what, if any, advantage a country with limited managerial skills and limited administrative capacity derives from organizing industrial activities under governmental control rather than through reliance on the competitive market place.

Two other examples are drawn from the area of international economic relations. In commercial policy, developing countries generally place great emphasis on policies of substituting domestic production for imports when the economics of the situation would indicate that economic efficiency would best be served by reliance on the principle of comparative advantage. And in almost all the developing countries and new nations, there is strong opposition to the investment of foreign capital and to the employment of foreign scientific, technical, and managerial personnel, even though capital and professional people are scarce and their scarcity frequently constitutes the major bottleneck in the process of economic development. Both phenomena are clearly derived from nationalism.

The problem these examples pose for the economist as social scientist is to explain the tenacity with which these policies are followed and the regularities of behavior that can be discerned among countries, in terms of an underlying logical connection running from nationalism to economic policy. The purpose of this article is to provide such an explanation in the form of a theoretical model of economic nationalism in new and developing states; the intention is not to pass judgment on the wisdom or otherwise of nationalist policies, but rather to explain such policies as a rational and economic response to certain types of situations.

The theoretical model presented derives primarily from three recent applications of economic theory to problems hitherto not generally considered to fall within its range.[1] The first of these is Gary S. Becker's study of discrimination against Negroes in the United States.[2] The key concept of this work is the "taste for discrimination," the notion that people who discriminate are willing to sacrifice material gain — by paying higher prices or accepting lower prices in their economic transactions — in order to enjoy a psychological gain derived from avoiding contact with the group discriminated against. The model of nationalism presented here adopts from Becker's work the notion that individuals seek — in accordance with the postulates of economic theory — to maximize their satisfaction, but that this satisfaction includes enjoyment of both psychic income and material income; it simply substitutes for the taste for discrimination a taste for nationalism.

The second source of the model is Anthony Downs' application of economic theory to the processes and practices of democratic

---

[1] The model also owes something to my earlier attempts to understand the origins of the particular policies recommended by Canadian nationalists in recent years; see my "Problems of Canadian Nationalism," Chap. 2 in *The Canadian Quandary* (Toronto: McGraw-Hill of Canada, 1963), and "Economic Nationalism in Canadian Policy," Chap. 6, below.

[2] Gary S. Becker, *The Economics of Discrimination* (Chicago: University of Chicago Press, 1957).

B

government.[3] Downs' basic hypothesis is that political parties seek to maximize their gains from office, but that they win office by catering to the preferences of the voters and can continue in office only by satisfying the voters' preferences for various types and quantities of governmental activity. In other words, power is exchanged for desired policies in a political transaction between party and electorate. A strategic element in Downs' theory of the workings of democracy is the cost of acquiring information. Downs uses this cost to explain the reliance on persuasion in arriving at political decisions, the inequality of political influence, the role of ideology, electoral apathy, and the bias of democratic government toward serving producer rather than consumer interests.

The third source of the model is Albert Breton's analysis of the economics of nationalism.[4] Breton identifies nationality with ownership by nationals of various types of property, and regards it as a type of collective consumption capital that yields an income of utility and can be invested in by spending public funds on the acquisition of such capital. Using this framework, Breton produces a number of specific and testable propositions about nationalism: nationalist policy is mainly concerned with redistributing income rather than with increasing it; specifically, the redistribution is from the working class to the middle class; consequently, where the working class is poor, there will be a tendency to resort to confiscation rather than the purchase of property. Furthermore, nationalism will tend to favor investment in national manufacturing, since manufacturing jobs and ownership are preferred by the middle class; its collective nature will appeal to socialists; and its emergence will be correlated with the rise of new middle classes who have difficulty in finding suitable career opportunities.

The development of the model of economic nationalism starts from Downs' model of the working of democracy. It is posited that political parties are engaged in the business of exchanging governmental policies and services — from which a party in power derives benefits in the form of psychic and material gains of various kinds — for votes from the electorate. The party's success in gain-

[3] Anthony Downs, "An Economic Theory of Political Action in a Democracy," *Journal of Political Economy*, LXVI (1957), 135–50; *An Economic Theory of Democracy* (New York: Harper, 1957).
[4] Albert Breton, "The Economics of Nationalism," *Journal of Political Economy*, LXXII (1964), 376–86.

ing and keeping power depends on its success in furnishing what the electorate desires from the government in exchange for its votes. The main obstacle to efficiency in this exchange stems from ignorance on both sides about the prospective gains from the policies offered and the cost of acquiring the information necessary to make the exchange efficient. This obstacle forces the political party to depend for its information about voter preferences on pressure groups and lobbyists, and on the communications media. Also, though Downs does not develop the point because he is primarily concerned with established democracies, this dependence gives the political parties a strong incentive to gain control over communications media as a means of establishing political control.

The average voter, however, is motivated by his own rational self-interest not to acquire much knowledge about the policies of political parties and their consequences for his economic welfare, because whether or not he is well informed he will have a negligible influence on which party is elected. It is this that gives ideology a crucial role in political life. The establishment of a distinctive party ideology simplifies the party's problem of communicating with the electorate by enabling the party to summarize all of its policies in one general symbolism; and it simplifies the problem of the voter, who can vote by ideology instead of being obliged to weigh up each party's record and promises on the whole range of specific policy issues. Parties will therefore compete largely through their ideologies.

In well-established democracies, the type of party system that emerges from this competition will depend on a variety of features, including the distribution among voters of ideological preferences, type of election system (whether by proportional representation or by plurality), and the geographical distribution of voter preferences. Proportional representation will tend to foster a multiplicity of ideologically differentiated parties; whereas plurality election will promote a two-party system, except where ideological difference is associated with geographical region. Actual policy in a multi-party system will, however, represent a compromise among ideologies owing to the necessity of forming coalitions to command power. In a two-party system the relation of party ideologies will be determined by the distribution of voter preferences for ideologies: if voters tend to group around a central ideological position (the distribution of voter preferences is unimodal), party ideologies will tend to be virtually indistinguishable. If, on the other hand, voter preferences group around two or more typical positions (the distribution of voter preferences is multimodal) and voters refrain from voting if party ideology departs too far from their own ideological preferences, party ideologies will be significantly differentiated; such a situation, however, may make the country politically unstable and threaten political disintegration.

Where democracy is not well established, there will be a strong incentive for a party to attempt to create a comprehensive and preclusive ideology to enable it to enjoy exclusive control of government; this will be especially so in an underdeveloped economy and society. The change of office from party to party in a normal democracy is an economically wasteful process, and relies on the capacity of the socio-political and economic system to reabsorb ousted political office holders without imposing great private losses on them. In an economically underdeveloped country, the change of office between parties is likely to impose substantial economic losses on the individuals who have to wait their turn in office, by comparison with the power and the material gains they would enjoy if they controlled the government permanently. The acceptance of normal democracy depends on acceptance of the rules of the game, but the acceptance rests not only on a democratic tradition but also on an economic and socio-political system that does not impose severe economic losses on political losers.

Nationalistic feeling provides a foundation for the establishment of a preclusive ideology as a prerequisite for one-party government; there is an evident connection between the stridency of nationalism in the new nations and their propensity to establish one-party government. Even where the two-party system is maintained, the competition in ideology would tend to make both parties stress nationalism and nationalist policies if there were widespread nationalist sentiment among the electorate. Only if there were a sharp division of voter preferences, with some voters envisaging serious disadvantages, would there be significant political division on the issue; in this case the political stability of the country would be seriously threatened.

Finally, one of Downs' important conclusions is that the working of political democracy will display an asymmetry with respect to economic issues. This asymmetry arises from the concentration of producer interests and the dispersion of consumer interests. The relevance of this asymmetry for nationalism is that nationalist policies tend to concentrate on specific producer interests, whereas their costs are dispersed thinly over the mass of consumers, so that it is not too difficult for nationalist policies to win political support on the basis of the producer gains they promise, even though the net benefits, taking consumers and producers together, are negative.

The foregoing argument has outlined an approach to the working of political democracy and party government and has attempted to integrate nationalism in developing countries with it. The next problem is the nature of nationalism as an ideology and of its political action program.

As an ideology or state of political feeling, nationalism can be conceived of, along the lines of the Becker analysis of discrimination against Negroes, as attaching utility or value to having certain jobs held or certain property owned by members of the national group rather than by non-members of the national group. (The difference between the two concepts, though this is a difference largely of degree rather than of kind, is that the utility accrues to members of the national group whether or not they themselves hold the jobs or the property in question; the consequences of this difference are elaborated subsequently.) In this context, it is most useful to employ a broad definition of property ownership, one which includes in "property" not merely the ownership of physical or financial assets but also rights to certain kinds of jobs, since job opportunities are property in the sense of yielding a stream of income to the holder. Nationalism can accordingly be conceived of as a state of social psychology or political sentiment that attaches value to having property in this broad sense owned by members of the national group.

The question that immediately arises is, "To what kinds of property does this utility of nationality become attached?" Clearly, in some sense it is the "important" or prestigious or socially relevant kinds of property that acquire this added value. One such, obviously, is the result of cultural and artistic activities — the national literature, music, and drama. Another is positions of authority in the governmental apparatus and in the social structure. Still another comprises particular types of economic activity and economic roles that carry superior status (and usually superior income also).

A related question is, "What determines which specific items of property acquire added value from nationalism?" There seem to be two major ways in which nationalistic utility can be acquired. One is internal, through observation within the country of foreign operations there; the property yielding income and status to the foreigner becomes the property valued by the nationalists. This mechanism of generating nationalistic utility is particularly important in formerly colonial countries or countries where foreign investment and alleged "economic imperialism" have been significant, where nationalism seeks particularly to replace the officialdom of the colonial power and the executives and shareholders of the foreign enterprises with nationals. The other mechanism is external, through contact with and observation of other nations, that provides knowledge of what forms of property are highly regarded in such societies.

Both of these mechanisms involve the determination of the nationalistic values of specific forms of property by imitation or emulation of other countries, either of their actual practices or of the "image" of themselves they project abroad. The importance of international emulation in determining nationalistic objectives is evident in a variety of areas. Examples in the field of economic policy have already been provided. Examples in other fields readily come to mind, such as the importance frequently attached to the winning of Olympic medals by a country's athletes or the tendency of the allocation of resources for scientific research in the more advanced countries to be dominated by the spectacular accomplishments of other countries.

The next step in the analysis is to recognize that the benefits from the gratification of nationalist sentiment are of two sorts: particular and general, or tangible and intangible. The particular benefits are the incomes and prestige that accrue to those nationals who acquire the property rights or the offices and employment opportunities in which nationalism invests. The general benefits consist of the psychic satisfaction derived by the community at large from gratification of the taste for nationalism. It is important to notice here the concentration of the tangible benefits on the subgroup of nationals eligible to hold the property or to fill the positions, as distinguished from the dispersion of the intangible benefits, which presumably accrue to the whole national society insofar as its members share the taste for nationalism. It is the intangible benefits which give national ownership of property the character of a collective consumption good — one for which consumption by one individual does not preclude consumption by another — and for the economist raise the difficult problem of how to determine the optimal quantity to supply.

The tangible benefits are directly or indirectly economic and are of considerable value to the individuals who may receive them; thus the bias of the democratic process toward producer interests becomes relevant. These individuals have an economic incentive to pursue these prospective benefits through the cultivation of nationalism. Further, given the mechanisms by which nationalistic utility becomes attached to specific items of property, these items will tend to be such as to yield tangible benefits primarily to the educated, the entrepreneurially qualified classes, some at least of the wealthy, and other elite groups, so that there is an inherent class slant to the economic interest in pursuing nationalism.

There is, moreover, a natural consilience of the strictly economic interests in nationalism and the cultural interests in nationalism. Both the intellectuals engaged in cultural activities and the owners and managers of communications media have an interest in nationalism, particularly when it can be combined with a linguistic difference, but even when it cannot, because nationalism creates a monopolistic barrier to competition from other countries' purveyors of the same sorts of cultural products. Thus cultural nationalism complements economic nationalism, both involving tangible benefits in the form of protection of the market for the services of individuals. This consideration suggests also that the strength of economic and cultural interests in nationalism will vary with the threat of competition and the need for protection of the market. One would expect to find nationalist sentiment strongest where the individuals concerned are most vulnerable to competition from foreign culture or from foreign economic activities; conversely, one would expect to find that the nations that are leading culturally and economically will tend to be internationalist and cosmopolitan in outlook, because this would tend to extend the market area for their cultural and economic products. These expectations accord broadly with experience.

We now turn from nationalism as a political ideology to nationalism as an economic program. As such, nationalism seeks to extend the property owned by nationals so as to gratify the taste for nationalism. There are a variety of methods available for accomplishing this objective.

One obvious method is confiscation — that is, the forced transfer of property from foreign owners to nationals. Here it is important to notice a certain ambiguity in the concept of confiscation, extremely useful to nationalists, which arises because what appears to be confiscation may not really be confiscation in the fundamental economic sense of the term. For example, nationalizing the civil service, or nationalizing the administrative and executive jobs in a particular enterprise, may appear to transfer property of value from the foreigners to the nationals. But insofar as the foreigners were receiving a fair price for their skilled qualifications, and nationalization involves replacing them with nationals of inferior skills at the same salaries, the effect is primarily to transfer income within the national group, toward the individuals favored with promotion at the expense of the general community which must bear the costs of poorer administration, inferior economic efficiency, or deterioration of the quality of the service that results.

The result of nationalizing jobs is not, of course, necessarily merely a transfer of income among nationals. If previously there has been genuine discrimination against nationals — for example, where the civil servants have been of a foreign nationality even though their jobs could be performed as efficiently or more efficiently by nationals available at lower salaries — there will be a genuine transfer of income from foreigners to nationals, since discrimination against nationals in employment gives foreigners a source of monopoly gain at the expense of nationals. It is always difficult to determine, however, whether the employment of non-nationals represents discrimination against nationals or reflects their inferior quality; under competitive conditions there is a presumption in favor of the latter assumption. The possibility of discrimination apart, nationalizing jobs is a matter of transferring income among members of the national group, with side effects in reducing aggregate real income by reducing the efficiency of performance. Genuine confiscation, which transfers valuable property from foreigners to nationals, is therefore largely confined to property in the narrow sense, that is, to the tangible wealth —

cash, securities, real property, and enterprises — owned in the country by foreigners.

The alternative to confiscation is investment of resources or purchase, that is, the use of wealth or savings that otherwise would be available for other purposes to purchase material property or job opportunities for nationals. This may be effected directly through public investment or indirectly through various policies influencing private investment. The public investment method includes both the nationalization of existing foreign enterprises with fair compensation and the use of development funds or public revenue to create new enterprises. The method of influencing private investment involves using tariffs and related policies to stimulate industries of the kind desired; these policies also entail public investment, in the sense that the use of the tariff, for example, involves imposing a tax on the consumer in the form of higher prices, the revenue from which goes to subsidize the creation of the protected enterprises by the private entrepreneurs who then receive the higher prices.

It must be recognized, of course, that nationalism is not the only reason why a government may choose to adopt any of these policies. There are many economic arguments about why such policies might be beneficial in terms of increasing the national income rather than serving purely to gratify the taste for nationalism. The relevant economic analysis is quite elaborate. It runs in terms of divergences between the private and the social costs of or returns from various kinds of investment, and includes such possibilities as: rationalizing the system of production by consolidation of control; training the entrepreneurial and laboring forces and so obtaining social benefits that private competition would not produce if left to itself (the infant industry argument); and obtaining cost reductions through exploiting economies of scale. These arguments are frequently effective in attracting support for nationalistic policies from non-nationalists, and especially socialists, who are inclined to believe implicitly that competition is inherently inefficient and susceptible of improvement by governmental action. The real question, however, is whether the facts of the situation conform to the possibilities of theoretical reasoning. Typically, little or no effort is devoted to confirming that this is so, the theoretical possibilities being employed instead to provide a plausible and apparently scientific defense of policies that are adopted for essentially nationalistic reasons.

With respect to the method of nationalization, it is necessary to realize that, provided compensation is fair, there is no transfer of wealth from foreigners to nationals, and no net gain in national wealth, because fair compensation involves paying the previous owner the present value of the future income he would have earned from the enterprise.[5] The only exception occurs when nationalization permits efficiency-increasing changes in production methods that the previous owner would not have introduced. The gain (or loss) from nationalization does not result from the mere fact of nationalization; instead, gains or losses are the result of changes in management methods and policies introduced after nationalization. Insofar as the objective of nationalization is to provide jobs for nationals, presumably people are employed in larger numbers or are of a lower quality than previously were employed, and this obviously involves economic waste.[6] Alternatively stated, potential national output is sacrificed in return for the psychic income obtained from greater employment of nationals. The same is true of public investment in the creation of new industries when such investment is influenced by the desire to provide high-income and high-status jobs for nationals.

The desire to provide more, and more worthy, jobs for nationals will influence the selection of industries for nationalization in certain ways, and this may incidentally provide a means of distinguishing nationalistic from socialistic nationalization.[7] "Nationalistic" nationalization, aside from the obvious tendency to concentrate on industries employing a high proportion of foreigners, will tend to be aimed at industries with a well-established and fairly static technology, that can be managed by bureaucratic routine, and at industries that enjoy a monopolistic position in the domestic market rather than competing actively in the domestic or especially the foreign market, since these characteristics will permit the employment of larger total numbers, and the substitution of lower-quality nationals for higher-quality foreigners, without risking the breakdown and bankruptcy of the industry. In any

[5] Breton makes unnecessarily heavy weather of this point.
[6] Again, there may be an economic gain rather than a loss, if previously nationals were discriminated against in the employment practices of the nationalized industry.
[7] I am indebted for this point to Professor A. D. Scott.

case, public ownership of industry, whether achieved by nationalization or new investment, permits losses incurred in consequence of the pursuit of nationalistic policies to be underwritten, within limits, by the taxing and borrowing powers of the government.

The alternative to investment or purchase of industry is the use of tariffs, tax concessions, and special privileges to promote the establishment of the kinds of industries that are desired. This method involves a much more clear-cut possibility of economic loss, through higher costs of production paid for by consumers in the form either of higher prices or of lost tax revenue that has to be made up either by other taxes or by reduced governmental services, and an overt transfer from the general consumer, who pays the higher prices or taxes or loses governmental services, to the favored producers who are given a protected position in the market. The use of the tariff or of tax concessions to induce the local establishment of particularly desired industries, however, frequently has the paradoxical result of increasing nationalist dissatisfaction, rather than of contributing to satisfaction, by inducing the foreign producer of a product previously imported to establish domestic production facilities in the country — with the result that the country exchanges the dissatisfaction of not having the industry in the country for the dissatisfaction of having its industry owned and staffed by foreign enterprises.[8]

The major implications of the theory of nationalist economic policy presented in this article may now be briefly summarized.

One implication is that nationalism will tend to direct economic development policy along certain specific lines; these lines might represent economic optimality, and would do so if the conditions posited by some familiar economic arguments were present. Failing empirical validation of those arguments, however, the consequence will be a reduction of material production below the economy's potential. In the first place, nationalist economic policy will tend to foster activities selected for their symbolic value in terms of concepts of national identity and the economic content

[8] This consequence of the tariff has been an important factor in the exacerbation of nationalist sentiment in Canada in recent years. The formation of the European Economic Community similarly has fostered American investment within the Community's boundaries and thereby provoked nationalist complaints.

of nationhood; in particular, emphasis will be placed on manufacturing; and, within manufacturing, on certain industries possessing
special value symbolic of industrial competence (such as the steel
and automotive industries). Second, nationalist economic policy
will foster activities offering prestigious jobs for the middle class
and/or the educated class; the nature of such activities varies with
the stage of development: very undeveloped countries favoring
bureaucratic jobs offering steady incomes for routine work; more
advanced countries favoring managerial and professional jobs
suitable for the products of the educational system; fairly mature
countries favoring jobs in higher education and research.[9] Third,
nationalism will tend to favor both extensive state control over
and extensive public ownership of economic enterprises; state
control provides employment for the educated directly, in the
central control system, while both the control system and public
ownership give the government social control over the allocation
of jobs to nationals.

Another implication is that nationalism will tend to direct economic policy toward the production of psychic income in the form
of nationalistic satisfaction at the expense of material income.

If attention is confined to material income alone, a third implication is that nationalism will tend to redistribute material income
from the lower class toward the middle class, and particularly toward the educated middle class; in this respect, nationalism reinforces the trend of modern society toward the establishment of a
class structure based on educational attainment.[10] This last implication relates to material income only, and does not necessarily
imply that the lower classes are worse off because of nationalism
when both real and psychic income are reckoned into the account.
It is quite possible that the psychic enjoyment that the mass of the
population derive from the collective consumption aspects of na-

[9] The emphasis on education in contemporary development theory tends to
produce a rat-race in which a country first invests a great deal of scarce capital
in educating people, and then is obliged to invest a great deal more in providing suitable employment opportunities for them, the consequence being a
double waste of resources. Sometimes needs for both more education and better jobs for the educated are urged simultaneously, despite the implicit
economic contradiction.

[10] It is one of the paradoxes of modern social philosophy that redistribution of income from the intellectually poor to the intellectually rich is regarded as desirable and proper, whereas redistribution from the materially
poor to the materially rich is regarded as utterly inequitable.

tionalism suffices to compensate them for the loss of material income imposed on them by nationalistic economic policies, so that nationalistic policies arrive at a quite acceptable result from the standpoint of maximizing satisfaction. It may even be that nationalistic policies are the cheapest and most effective way to raise real income in less developed countries;[11] in some cases, one suspects, the prospects for genuine economic growth are so bleak that nationalism is the only possible means available for raising real income.[12]

It would seem, however, from the economic analysis of government presented earlier, that the lower classes are unlikely to be net gainers from economic nationalism, owing to the effects of ignorance and the costs of acquiring information in concentrating political power in the hands of pressure groups, and the general tendency for producer interests to dominate over consumer interests that results from the natural response of voters to the high cost and negligible value of acquiring political information. The tendency for the mass of the population to suffer losses from economic nationalism is probably reinforced in the new nations by the prevalence of systems of one-party government, in which the party is based largely on urban support and frequently exercises a virtual monopoly over the country's communications system.[13]

Even though nationalism may involve a substantial redistribution of real income toward the middle class at the expense of the mass of the population, this redistribution may perform a necessary function in the early stages of forming a nation, in the sense that the existence of a substantial middle class may be a prerequi-

[11] This point was suggested by Professor Burton Weisbrod.

[12] Field research by members of the Committee for the Comparative Study of New Nations suggests that this may in fact be the case in some of the new African nations. Nationalism may itself create such a situation, nationalistic economic policies blocking economic growth so effectively that it becomes necessary to resort to ever more extreme nationalistic sentiment and policy to maintain the illusion of economic development.

[13] Both dependence on urban support and control over communications media are logical consequences of the economic theory of government as applied to such countries. Dependence on urban support in turn reinforces the bias of development policy toward promotion of manufacturing, and in general fosters policies favoring the city dweller at the expense of the agricultural population. A particular aspect of this, important especially in Latin America, is the maintenance of low urban transport rates by direct or indirect subsidization, which in its turn fosters urban population growth and increases the political importance of urban residents.

site of a stable society and democratic government. In other words, an investment in the creation of a middle class, financed by resources extracted from the mass of the population by nationalistic policies, may be the essential preliminary to the construction of a viable national state. This problem, however, belongs in the spheres of history, sociology, and political science rather than economics.

2. NINETEENTH-CENTURY EUROPEAN EXPERIENCE WITH POLICIES OF ECONOMIC NATIONALISM

Arcadius Kahan

Wherever in a new Economy a discernible direction of development can be detected which possesses similarities with older ones, we have a valuable yardstick for comparison in the experience of the more mature economies.

Wilhelm Roscher, 1843

When analyzing and describing manifestations of economic nationalism, one ought not to consider the whole set of economic measures designed directly to strengthen the nation's political and military power, like large state expenditures on the maintenance of a military establishment and police force.[1] Although such expenditures are an integral part of a national or nationalistic policy, they do not constitute policies of economic nationalism as usually defined. By the same token, policies as diverse as the Navigation Acts and the Continental blockade or Continental system and those of extreme economic warfare ought to be excluded from the discussion.

I shall also not concern myself with the extremely interesting problem of colonialism as an expression of nineteenth-century economic nationalism, since this topic would require a much more detailed treatment than the format of this essay allows.

ECONOMIC NATIONALISM AND THE PROMOTION OF ECONOMIC GROWTH

An initial problem in the analysis of economic nationalism is to establish the relationship between economic nationalism and the promotion of economic growth. In the economic policies of the presently emerging states the coincidence of the two appears almost to be taken for granted. But this was not necessarily the case in Europe during the nineteenth century; and where it was the case, accelerated economic development appeared to be a means

[1] Military appropriations were at a maximum, relative to the total state budget, during the eighteenth century in continental Europe. However, it would be improper to attribute the volume of such expenditures to policies of economic nationalism.

17

for the achievement of ultimate nationalistic goals, and not an independent goal in itself. And although to say that economic development is a means rather than a goal does not explain much, at least it indicates that, within the framework of nationalist ideology and policy, economic development cannot be treated either as a self-contained entity or as the cornerstone of general nationalist policy. In addition, economists would be wrong to expect any marked degree of consistency and rationality in policies designed to induce economic growth.[2] Very few made such demands in nineteenth-century Europe.

That nationalistic ideology and the objective of economic development (as presently understood in terms of industrialization) might at times conflict is clearly illustrated by two quotations from the classical representative of the German protectionist school, Professor Adolph Wagner.

> An adequate protection for agriculture, higher than the present, would be in the general interest of the whole community, even if by its means the industrial development of the state and possibly also the growth of population should be not entirely stopped, but certainly slackened. . . . The maintenance of a production capability of German agriculture is vital for the maintenance of the German people now and for the future.[3]
> It is not to be denied that, like all the great things which a nation needs — armaments, civil administration, justice, a system of education, arrangements for the care of the economic interests of the community, etc. — so also the maintenance of the permanent economic and numerical strength of the nation through an adequate and sturdy agrarian population requires sacrifices. But we believe these sacrifices, in this case as in the others, are necessary for that higher objective which we have in view.[4]

In contrast to contemporary nationalists in the developing countries, Wagner stressed the necessity of protection of agriculture in the preservation of the nation. More important for our analysis is

[2] The term "rationality" is used in this context synonymously with the concept of economic efficiency. Economists generally believe that although the goals of optimal economic efficiency and rapid economic growth are conceptually not mutually exclusive, one is often sacrificed for the sake of the other in practical experience.

[3] A. Wagner, *Agrar und Industriestaat* (Jena: G. Fischer, 1901), pp. 2, 3.
[4] *Ibid.*, p. 25.

his general proposition that national interests, however defined, are of a higher order of priority than the demands of economic rationality or of economic development.

The distinction between nationalist policy and the promotion of development was recognized by another German economist, Gustav Schmoller, who wrote at the close of the nineteenth century:

> So Russia, the United States and France have fallen into a highly protective system, and sometimes into a commercial policy, which though it aims at international power, is of a worse kind, and hinders the economic development of these countries instead of promoting it.[5]

Thus it would appear necessary to distinguish between the adoption of nationalist objectives and the assignment of high priority to economic development. I would suggest, as a general hypothesis, the proposition that, although economic backwardness has always been considered detrimental to the advancement of nationalist interests,[6] it was chiefly the development of new military technology requiring an elaborate and modern industrial base that demanded a forced pace of industrialization and thus elevated economic growth to prominence among the objectives of nationalism in nineteenth-century Europe. In other words, the emergence of industrialization as a major goal of nationalism was the consequence of the military needs and objectives of national states, not of any belief in the desirability of industrialization per se.

THE PHILOSOPHICAL BASIS OF NATIONALISTIC ECONOMIC POLICIES IN THE NINETEENTH CENTURY

In my treatment of nationalist economic policies in nineteenth-century Europe, I shall first indicate briefly the nature of these policies and then examine their impact on the economic growth of the major countries adopting them. I will assume that economic nationalism is based on two propositions that, for brevity, may be stated as follows:

---

[5] G. Schmoller, *Jahrbuch für Gesetzgebung Verwaltung und Volkswirtschaft* (Leipzig, 1902), Part II, p. 353.

[6] An exception to the general view was provided by some Russian statesmen during the nineteenth century who were in favor of preserving the elements of economic backwardness in order to prevent "the corruption of the Russian soul by the Western value system."

C

1. American Motors is better for the United States than British Motors and therefore deserves support;
2. What is good for the United States is good for American Motors.

Historically, these two propositions emerged in that order, at least with respect to their influence on economic policies, and coincided with two phases or periods of economic nationalism. The order was reversed as regards the evolution of the intellectual underpinnings of economic nationalism and of economic thought.

The intellectual roots of economic nationalism are to be sought on the one hand in the development of political theory or philosophy, and on the other hand in the reaction to classical economic analysis as laid down by Adam Smith. I shall be concerned only with the latter.

It is an old truism, which nevertheless ought to be repeated, that Adam Smith's economics rested upon the principles of "natural law" and rationalism, on which bases individualistic economic activity, ethics, and law could be harmonized.

The reaction against Smith's ahistorical, cosmopolitan, and "natural" concepts, which ignored particulars for the sake of the general, came first from the "romantic school" represented by Adam Müller [7] and later from the German historical school. For obvious reasons, the reaction against Smith and the classical political economy could not be directed purely against the economic analysis, but had to include a reexamination of the underlying principles and thus in effect became a part of the reaction against the philosophy of the eighteenth-century Enlightenment.

> Müller viewed the economy not necessarily as the commercial struggle of atomized interests . . . but as an aspect of the activity of a commonwealth, as a supra-individual relationship (superseding individuals) that does not follow mechanistic laws; a market, according to Müller, is not exclusively a meeting place for the exchange of commodities into money-equivalents, but also is an outlet for relations between humans. . . . [Economic activity] is a part of the totality of *physical and*

[7] Adam Müller, *Elemente der Staatskunst*, Vol. I, 1809. See also D. Vikor, *Economic Romanticism in the Twentieth Century* (New Delhi: New Book Society of India, 1964), pp. 23–33.

See Walter J. Fischel, "Der Historismus in der Wirtschaftwissenschaft," *Vierteljahresschrift für Sozial und Wirschaftsgeschichte*, Vol. 47 (Wiesbaden, 1960), pp. 1–31.

spiritual forces of the nation in the change and continuity of generations. . . . [While for Smith] the human being was essentially an individual, [for Müller] he is basically a citizen; therefore, in one concept of the economy the creative activity originates with the individual and spreads within the economy . . . while in the second case the movement is a reciprocal process . . . every individual produces the society, while society produces also the individual citizen.[8]

Friedrich List, a forerunner of the German historical school who probably borrowed more from Müller than from Hamilton, continued the attack against the classical school, which he considered to suffer from three basic weaknesses.

The system of the [classical] school suffers from three major shortcomings. First, from a groundless *cosmopolitanism*, which both ignores the nature of the nation and does not take into consideration the satisfaction of its interests. Second, from a deadly *materialism*, which emphasizes the exchange value of commodities and largely ignores spiritual and political, present and future interests as well as the productive forces of the nation. Third a disorganizing *particularism* and *individualism*, which while denying the socialized nature of labor and the impact of cooperation of efforts and their consequences of a higher order, basically describes private activity only, [it describes] how [private activity] is developing through a free exchange with society (meaning the whole of humanity), as though the latter is not divided into separate national entities.

Between the individual and humanity there is the nation . . . it is only through the nation and within the nation that the individual can receive spiritual training, achieve productive force, security and welfare; and therefore the civilization of humanity is possible and can be understood only through the civilization and development of nations.[9]

In his criticism of the classical school List was supported by Roscher and other members of the German historical school.[10]

[8] Hans Freyer, *Die Bewertung der Wirtschaft im Philosophischen Denken des 19. Jahrhunderts* (Leipzig, 1921), pp. 52, 53.

[9] Friedrich List, *Das nationale System der politischen Oekonomie*, 1857, pp. 153–54.

[10] Roscher wrote in 1843: "How national wealth ought to be augmented is also for us a major problem; [its solution] is, however, not our primary con-

Parenthetically, it may be observed that Marx, who was trained in the German philosophy but embraced the classical economics, displayed in his economic writing some affinity with the criticisms brought by the historical school against classical economics. Consider the phrase "the capitalist system presents the relation between producers as the exchange of commodities": substitute "national interests" for "class interests" in the Marxian analysis and you have, prima facie, an echo of some of the criticism leveled against the classical school mentioned above.

Thus to summarize the new tone of the early criticisms of the classical school of political economy, one could perhaps say that the critics viewed the economy as a social institution shaped only to a small extent by the direct economic interests of its individual participants and to a much greater extent by the traditions, spirit, culture, and historical conditioning of large distinguishable and defined groups, like nations, classes, etc.

PROTECTIONIST ECONOMIC POLICIES IN THE NINETEENTH CENTURY AND THEIR EFFECTIVENESS

However, since it is at the level, not of ideas, but of economic policies, that I propose to test the relevance of European nineteenth-century experience, I shall proceed with an examination of the policies themselves. There is a basic difference in the process of policy choice between the developing countries of the twentieth century and those of the nineteenth century. The developing countries of the twentieth century take as their point of departure some model of political and economic organization, and a set of goals representing a certain level of economic welfare, all of them derived from their image of the future. The major problem, then, is to adopt methods that will reduce as much as possible the time interval between the present and the point of attainment of the goals. Economic nationalism therefore becomes a part of the system of goals as well as an instrument for reducing the time interval.

In nineteenth-century continental Europe, neither was economic nationalism a prominent component of the set of goals, nor

cern. Our goal is to present what the nations thought about their economies; what they wanted and experienced; what they desired and achieved; why they desired it and how they achieved it." Wilhelm Roscher, *Grundriss zu Vorlesungen über die Staatswirtschaft* (Gottingen, 1843), p. iv.

did the European nations subscribe to the notion of a timetable for the achievement of over-all economic objectives.

I have already ventured the generalization that during the nineteenth century the adoption of economic policies based upon a preference for domestic products over foreign, and for domestic branches of the economy over foreign branches, preceded the espousal of the principle that, over all, national interest ought to override particular interests within the country. In other words, nationalist economic policies historically developed from policies furthering particular or group interests to policies epitomizing an over-all view of the national interest.

In my judgment, nineteenth-century economic policies repre· sented by and large the first of these two stages of economic nationalism. Protectionism is one of the earliest forms of economic nationalism. To the extent that the protectionist policies of the nineteenth century were nationalistically motivated, therefore, they deserve our attention. In this connection the German experience, supplemented by details of the Italian experience, provides an exemplar of the experience of such policies on the European continent.[11]

The classic characterization of the German experience was provided by Gustav Schmoller:

> All protective movements are closely connected with national sentiments, strivings after international authority, efforts toward the balance of power, and therefore will continue to exist so long as amongst the fully developed states there are others striving after economic development, and so long as the people for economic purposes have need of every weapon that stands ready for their use.[12]

But Schmoller was also able to detect some shortcomings in the policy of protectionism:

> This new period of protectionism, this neomercantilism, has come not because the theorists and statesmen were incapable of understanding the lofty arguments of Free Trade,

[11] The use of protectionist measures by Germany and Italy is no accident, but would fit our understanding of protectionism as a measure of economic nationalism at a certain phase of its development. One is also reminded of the fact that the process of national unification of Germany and Italy took place in the nineteenth century.

[12] Gustav Schmoller, in "Verhandlungen des Vereins für Socialpolitik," *Schriften des Vereins für Socialpolitik* (1902), pp. 264–71.

not because everywhere some monopolists and large manufacturers control the government, but out of natural nationalist tendencies, particularly in those countries with the most
liberal and democratic constitutions. It is based not alone or
even chiefly on the doctrine of "educational tariffs" [the infant
industry doctrine of List] but arises out of an instinctive,
rather than reasoned, conviction that the tariffs are an international weapon which, skillfully employed, can be of the
utmost use.

Admittedly this neomercantilism frequently overlooks the
fact that these weapons may be used unskillfully and mis-
takenly as often as rightly.[13]

It is possible to distinguish in the German experience two distinct periods that can be termed periods of economic protectionism. One took place during the 1830's and 1840's, and the other
began in the 1880's. They were different in their intensity and in
their quality.

It is even difficult to label the protectionism of the 1830's and
1840's as nationalistic. The idea of nationalism was in fact anath-
ema (owing to the liberal and democratic connotation of the term
nationalism prevailing during this period) to the chief beneficiary
of the policies of the *Zollverein* — the absolutist Kingdom of Prus-
sia. In addition, the state economic policy that followed the 1848
Revolution could be described as liberal and leaning toward free
trade. The Cobden Treaty of 1860 between England and France
was followed by a number of treaties to which Germany became
a partner, and the most-favored-nation clause was invariably a
part of the treaty provisions.

A lowering of tariffs followed until well into the 1870's, but the
adverse economic effects on Germany of the business cycle down-
turn that started in 1873 were accentuated by the fact that, owing
to the same cyclical phenomenon, British metals and textiles
became relatively cheaper than before. In addition, a decisive
factor in bringing about a change in German policies was the
situation of German agriculture, and particularly the competition
between German and United States grain. Germany changed
from a grain exporter to a net grain importer, largely because of
the high cost of intensive German agriculture in comparison with

[13] G. Schmoller, *Jahrbuch für Gesetzgebung, Verwaltung und Volkswirtschaft* (1902), Part II, p. 353.

the low cost of extensive American production of grain. While Bismarck and the Prussian Junkers were originally free-traders (similar in their attitude to that of the American South in that period), their position changed after the agricultural depression. The change was sudden and was signaled in political terms by the resignation in 1876 of Rudolph Delbrück, the chief architect of the German economic policy. The Tariff Act was introduced in 1879; it embraced a tariff on agricultural products and on iron and other industrial products, and increased the tariff on textiles.

Nevertheless, by later standards the tariff rates were not very high. For example, the wheat and rye tariff was actually only 5 per cent ad valorem, and although it was later increased (when it turned out to be insufficient to protect domestic production and prevent a decrease of domestic prices), it nevertheless compares favorably with later tariff rates.[14] The German tariff of 1879 provided a subsidy for the grain producers, but did not cause much harm to the cause of industrialization because the price of grain in Germany continued to drop in spite of the tariff. The fall of Bismarck and the period of the Caprivi government witnessed some attempts to mitigate the tariffs in the hope that other countries would follow suit. As a result of a further decline in the price of grain and a new wave of protectionist agitation, the Caprivi government fell and the protectionist policy was resumed. But by and large, in comparison with the tariffs of the United States, France, Russia, and Austria, the level of the German tariff was not very high and therefore not very detrimental in its effects. During the whole period prior to World War I, the Germans, although relying heavily upon the tariff, did not turn to autarky as a national goal.[15]

Alexander Gershenkron has brilliantly analyzed the Italian experience.[16] He reaches the conclusion that it is more reasonable to regard the tariff as one of the obstacles in the path of Italian industrialization than to regard it as a real aid to that industrialization. He points out that Italy, which followed the trend toward a

[14] Gustav Stolper, *Deutsche Wirtschaft seit 1870* (Tübingen: J. C. B. Mohr, 1964), p. 42.

[15] *Ibid.*, p. 43.

[16] Alexander Gerschenkron, "Notes on the Rate of Industrial Growth in Italy, 1881–1913," *Journal of Economic History*, Vol. XV, No. 4 (December, 1955), p. 368.

protectionist policy for agricultural commodities common to all Europe, could ill afford to protect agriculture by comparison with Germany, and, as he says, never "should have dared to subject the tender plant of its industrial growth to the rigors of a protectionist climate in agriculture."

In Italian industry, the chief objects of protection were cotton textiles and ferrous metal-making, the first a relatively old industry with a somewhat aged technology and the latter an industry based upon low-grade ores and high-priced scarce coal resources. While supposedly the goal of the tariff was also to provide protection for the engineering-products industry, the basic assumption adopted — quite inexplicably in my judgment — was that an engineering industry has to be based upon a domestic iron and steel output. This is an early version of the steel-mill craze, familiar to observers of the newly developing countries at the present time. The interesting feature of Italian tariff policy in the 1880–95 period was that tariff rates were lowered for the engineering industries while they remained high for metallurgy and textiles. It is small wonder, therefore, that the spurt of Italian industrialization came only after the tariff policy was liberalized during 1896–97; only then did new branches of industry start to develop.

One would probably gain little additional insight by citing the French, Austro-Hungarian, or Russian experience in tariff policies. In fact, these experiences seem to cast further doubt on the general notion that protective policies by themselves made much difference to the pace of the process of economic change in Europe. To the extent that the tariffs protected agriculture, their impact was similar to that of the Corn Laws in England, and there is good reason to doubt that the Corn Laws aided the industrialization of that country. As far as the industrial tariffs are concerned, their income-distributive effects might have aided certain branches of industry; their over-all effectiveness depended to a considerable extent upon the range and choice of the industries to be protected. Some projections of industries that it would pay to protect turned out to be justified by subsequent developments, others not. Nevertheless, it should be mentioned (with all necessary caution) that, for the large countries, protective policies had some impact upon the pattern of regional development and probably contributed toward the formation and broadening of an internal market within the boundaries of these countries. To this extent, the nationalistic goals and, perhaps to a lesser extent, economic growth were served by protectionism.

In summary, one cannot reach any decisive conclusions about the effectiveness of the protectionist policies adopted by the European countries in the nineteenth century. It is obvious, however, that in some cases subsidies would probably have achieved much better results, especially if they had been concentrated on industries strategic for economic development.

OTHER ASPECTS OF NINETEENTH-CENTURY ECONOMIC NATIONALISM

It would, however, be wrong to assume that economic nationalism in nineteenth-century Europe was limited to protective policies only. In fact, there was a whole "arsenal" of weapons — to use Schmoller's phrase — to which both industrial entrepreneurs and governments resorted. One example of a nationalistic response by industrial entrepreneurs is provided by the emergence of cartels in Germany.

The explanation of the emergence of cartels during this period may, perhaps, be sought in the fact that this was an attempt on the part of the protected industries to maximize their profits up to the full amount of the margin provided by protection; whereas under competitive conditions in the internal market, the internal price might be below the ceiling set by the world market price and the tariff. Thus, such industries as coke, coal, and steel were protected and cartelized at the same time. One could certainly find very little evidence of distaste or resistance on the part of entrepreneurs entering cartel arrangements. To the extent that some of the domestic cartels developed into international ones — as did one of the earliest, the International Rail Makers Association (founded in 1883) — the participants claimed that they performed a nationally useful function by securing a share in the world output of the cartelized industry. Whether nationalist feelings were mitigated or intensified as a result of participation in an international cartel is a question that can be answered only by political scientists or by psychologists. I find the experience of cartelization in Europe of significance primarily because it provided a prototype for various monopolistic arrangements, licensing schemes, and other forms of production and distribution quota systems practiced in the emerging new nations. Needless to say, protection of inefficient producers is not the only consequence of such policies.

The evidence of the European experience does not warrant the conclusion that nationalism contributes substantially to the creation of the prerequisites of a modern, industrialized society. A social overhead of considerable size, which facilitated the use of potential labor and physical resources, may have been created on the European continent in some instances for nationalist reasons, so that nationalism served the subsequent purposes of economic development. But only to a very slight extent can one attribute to nationalism the creation of an indigenous managerial class and skilled labor force in continental Europe. Thus, during the earliest phase of nationalism, when the state used the industrial entrepreneurs, industrial firms, and industry branches as the main vehicles for furthering national aims, and policies were designed to aid these particular groups, the evidence of European experience is not clear-cut with regard to the effectiveness of nationalism in promoting the process of economic growth in its first phase.

THE SECOND PHASE OF ECONOMIC NATIONALISM

The second phase of economic nationalism, which I have described as the one during which the overriding principle becomes the proposition that what is good for the United States ought to be good for American Motors, has obviously much more affinity with the behavior of the new nations.[17] For this period, in particular for the early part of it, it is convenient to consider the relationship between nationalism and economic growth, with particular emphasis on the differences between decentralized and centralized patterns of economic growth. In other words, it appears that nationalistic policies were more frequently followed in cases where the need for centralized activity to support economic development was greater, or, to put it differently, centralized action was resorted to when nationalist feelings were strong and no substitutes for centralized actions were readily available. This obviously brings into the picture the role of the

[17] Some of the differences in the behavior of the developed and the developing countries at present could be explained by the lack of experience of the new nations with the "first phase" of economic nationalism.

state as an active participant in economic activity, taking over some functions previously reserved for the entrepreneur.

If we take the experience of Germany as an example, we note the emergence of attempts to expand state ownership and control over a wider area. Railroads are a case in point, and as a coincidence, but hardly an accident, the proposal to nationalize the railroads was accepted during the same year that the protective tariff was enacted in Germany (1879). Government participation in mining and heavy industry was accompanied by municipalization of public utilities, and municipal public utilities or mixed private-public companies became the prevailing form of ownership. The influence of the state (or government) in banking increased along with the growing involvement of banks in domestic industrial investment. The Reichsbank, although possessing private stockholders, was under the control of government-appointed managers; the Prussian state banks were growing; and the municipal savings banks had more deposits than all private commercial banks taken together. Although economic historians often contrast the Western and Eastern European patterns of development, and present the Central European pattern of economic growth as one in which the credit-generating institutions (the banks) took over some of the functions in the promotion of economic growth and industrialization that were performed in Eastern Europe by the state itself, the role of the state in the growth of the banking system in Central Europe should not be overlooked.

Thus, economic nationalism had some impact upon the creation of a more unified capital market and upon the direction of capital investment, or the process of channeling savings into investments. What further role economic nationalism had in promoting a higher rate of voluntary savings, or of imposing forced savings, is a complicated question. In the cases where policies to increase savings were promoted and carried out, the nationalist motivation was not always apparent. That nationalist tendencies were apparent in the area of foreign investment (either by governments or by private interests supported by governments) is beyond any doubt. The German, as well as the French, cases of foreign investments in Eastern Europe, the Balkans, and Turkey bear witness to that.

CONCLUDING REMARKS

In this paper I have discussed some of the European experience characterized by protectionist policies, by the process of cartelization or monopolization, and by establishing state control in various areas of economic life, and I have drawn what I consider a valid distinction between two phases of nationalist economic policies. From the historical perspective, the link between nationalism and industrialization became much stronger with the intensification of nationalism. And, if I may venture to hypothesize, the commitment to industrialize has gained in seriousness and strength because nationalism in the post-World War I period achieved a more durable fusion with radicalism than it had achieved previously. It is the infusion of radicalism that drives nationalism not only to the extreme of autarky vis-à-vis the outside world but also to the subordination of all group interests to the national interests, however defined. In order to understand certain economic policies and some fallacies of the new nations, we should not omit from our analysis the forces of radicalism, which assert that what is good for the United States is good, not only for American Motors, but also for the general public. In a certain sense Adam Smith's concept of natural harmony, which was attacked by the historical school, is being reinstated and reinforced by a radical regrouping of value structures derived not from "natural law" but from man-made laws and collectively determined social preferences.

3. ECONOMIC NATIONALISM IN BRITAIN IN THE NINETEENTH CENTURY

Roger W. Weiss

Economic policies that are nationalistic need not advance the economic well-being of the nation; expenditures for national defense, for example, consciously apply economic resources to uses that neither contribute consumer services nor add to productive capacity. Other policies inspired by a sense of nationalism may coincidentally reduce economic welfare. Limitation of economic activity within a country when conducted by foreign enterprises, limitation of investment in foreign enterprises abroad, or the limitation of employment of foreign workmen — all are examples which come to mind. Such policies, which fortuitously or intentionally sacrifice national economic well-being to other goals — national political security or cultural homogeneity — are not the concern of this chapter.

This chapter will deal with economic policies pursued out of a sense of national economic advantage. Free trade is such a policy. Those who advocated free trade in the first half of the nineteenth century expected the increased welfare of the nation — and incidentally, perhaps, of the rest of the world — to result. Policies regulating the export of capital, the admission of foreigners to trade in overseas territories under the political control of the British, and the regulation of the economic activity of subjects in the overseas empire, will be examined for the degree of advantage to the economic welfare of Britain they afforded, in the intentions of those who advocated or executed the policies. We will, in other words, examine the strength of the national economic motive in British policies.

Beyond economic nationalism in the regulation of foreign trade and investment and the relations between colonial members of the empire and the mother country, we must investigate areas of policy that relate less directly to economic well-being. Was British foreign policy directed consistently to advance Britain's economic interests? Was it neutral to British economic interests? Did it to a significant degree sacrifice British economic interests to consideration of power supremacy? Several examples are examined — the Crimean War, the Suez Canal purchase, and the imperial penetration of India and Nigeria.

Since careful analysis often reveals, and the silent working of powerful interests has often ensured, that policies have had effects that were not apparent in the rationalizations that were used in their defense, no study of the ends of policy could be complete without an examination of the realized effects of the policies. These may differ widely from the announced intentions. Even critics of British policy have often been misled by their failure to analyze the realized outcomes; those who criticized British free trade as peculiarly suited to British industrial dominance should have seen that protection would have better served Britain at such a time. Thus while free trade might have been intended as a self-serving national policy, it would still be true that the results benefited the rest of the world and did not maximize British national welfare. It might similarly be true that the subsequent retreat from free trade might have been intended to raise British welfare at the expense of foreigners; but, under the circumstances of the loss of British competitive advantage in industrial production, it reduced British welfare. Thus British intentions may have been nationalistic, but "realized" British policy was not.

By national interest or national welfare, we mean what might be quantified as national real income. In advocating free trade, Smith and Mill believed that the gains to the greater number of lower-class consumers of food would exceed the losses of the small number of landlords whose land rents would fall. The classical and utilitarian concept of national welfare — the greatest good for the greatest number — still serves as a welfare criterion and is what we shall take for national welfare. But the landlords, the exporting manufacturers, and the laborers and investors in foreign enterprises may have been the beneficiaries of policies that were defended in the national interest. Again, careful analysis must disentangle the true beneficiaries from the hypothecated ones before we can say whose interest British economic policy served. From a brief examination of a number of examples of policies, I conclude that while British policy was not advocated on grounds of the desirability of sacrificing the national well-being to that of foreigners, that policy served national ends only very imperfectly even in those cases where it served them at all. By comparison with twentieth-century practice, British policy in the nineteenth century was broadly cosmopolitan and to a large degree self-sacrificing.

The analysis of British economic policies below attempts to distinguish national from cosmopolitan benefit, intended from realized effects, national from sectional benefits, and the pursuit of economic welfare from the sometimes competing pursuit of political power.

Four aspects of British policy will be considered: (1) the policy of free trade; (2) the economic aspect of British foreign policy; (3) foreign investment policy; and (4) the policy of imperialism.

THE POLICY OF FREE TRADE

Before Adam Smith, British policy protected British agriculture against imports and protected British and colonial fishing and shipping interests by preferences and by the exclusion of foreign merchants from certain types of trade within the empire. Smith attempted to prove that such policies impoverished Britain by drawing resources away from their most productive use. Free trade was therefore consistent with Britain's national interests. Lionel Robbins, in his interesting lectures on *The Theory of Economic Policy*, is very emphatic:

> It must be realized that this consumption which was regarded as the end of economic activity was the consumption of a limited community, the members of the nation-state. To the extent to which they repudiated former maxims of economic warfare and assumed mutual advantage in international exchange, it is true that the outlook of the Classical Economists seems, and indeed is, more spacious and pacific than that of their antagonists. But there is little evidence that they often went beyond the test of national advantage as a criterion of policy, still less that they were prepared to contemplate the dissolution of national bonds. If you examine the ground on which they recommend free trade, you will find that it is always in terms of a more productive use of *national* resources: I do not think that Adam Smith's dictum that "defence . . . is of much more importance than opulence" was called in question by any of them. . . . All that I contend is that we get our picture wrong if we suppose that the English Classical Economists would have recommended, because it was good for the world at large, a measure which they thought

would be harmful to their own community. It was the consumption of the national economy which they regarded as the end of economic activity.[1]

Fortunately, there were few instances that required Smith to have to measure the welfare of Britain against that of the rest of the world, and he was therefore able to care for both without sacrificing either.

> The monopoly of the colony trade . . . like all the other mean and malignant expedients of the mercantile system, depresses the industry of all other countries but chiefly that of the colonies, without in the least increasing, but on the contrary diminishing, that of the country in whose favor it is established.[2]

Smith recommended freeing the American colonies. In this he was following the logic by which he showed that it was to the interest of neither the colonies nor Britain to retain the colonial relationship. But when Smith reflected that the ruling classes have a special interest in retaining control of the colonies as a matter of pride and for the patronage that the colonies could provide to their friends and allies, he offered an alternative solution: bring the colonies into the British constitution, allowing them to elect representatives in proportion to the taxes they pay to the imperial treasury. Smith was willing to contemplate the eventual subordination of Great Britain to the overseas colonies as they increased their population and wealth. His sense of nationality did not prevent him from giving this alternative his serious support; his economics, while not entirely free from considerations of national advantage, must be studied in relation to his version of nationalism, which was remarkably free from chauvinism.[3]

Britain did not immediately embark on free trade in spite of

---

[1] L. Robbins, *The Theory of Economic Policy in English Classical Political Economy* (London: Macmillan & Co., Ltd., 1961), p. 9.

[2] Adam Smith, *Wealth of Nations* (New York: Random House [Modern Library]), pp. 576–7.

[3] *Ibid.*, p. 589. While Smith recommended peaceful independence for Britain's American colonies, he did not object to their remaining in the empire and obtaining representation in Parliament. "There is not the least probability that the British constitution would be hurt by the union of Great Britain with her colonies. . . . The assembly which deliberates and decides concerning the affairs of every part of the empire, in order to be properly informed, ought certainly to have representatives from every part of it. That this union, however, could be easily effectuated . . . I do not pretend."

the popularity of Smith's economics. The enlightened statesman-
ship of Canning, Huskisson, Peel, and Gladstone succeeded in
reducing protection only gradually, until, in the emergency of the
Irish famine, the bold step that virtually freed trade could be
made. Gladstone, under whom duties on manufactured goods were
removed, defended free imports in a parliamentary debate.

> Suppose that 50,000 head of cattle were to be annually im-
> ported, such importation would produce but a small effect
> upon the prices of meat, but it would create an import trade
> to the amount of half a million of money, a trade which, in its
> nature, would lead by a smooth, certain course of operation,
> to an export trade in return, of an equal amount; which would
> contribute — he did not say in a moment, but in the course
> of years — to an increased demand for employment and
> labour.[4]

In addition to the policy of protection, Britain had a long-
standing policy of prohibiting the export of manufacturing machinery and also the emigration of skilled artisans. As late as
1825 and 1833 the prohibition of the export of specified machines
was renewed in legislation, and the Board of Trade appears to
have denied licenses for the export of such machinery as spinning-
frames and other textile equipment and certain machine tools.
But the prohibition applied only to specified pieces of machinery;
other machinery, either not on the list or invented after the legislation, was freely exported, and even the specified pieces were
smuggled out in boxes falsely labeled. But since the "export" of
artisans, drawings, and models could not be stopped, and foreign
visitors were free to observe industrial processes in England,
the export of technique and the foreign manufacture of pro-
hibited machinery could not be prevented. The intention to
control the export of machinery remained alive during the first
half of the century. It died with the conversion to free trade,
having been made anomalous by evasion and arbitrary application years before.[5]

When Britain's devotion to free trade declined, it did not fall
suddenly. Although Disraeli and his followers for years wanted
revenge and a revival of protection, the most they dared propose

[4] Hansard, *Parliamentary Reports*, LXIV (1842), 645.
[5] J. H. Clapham, *An Economic History of Modern Britain* (London: Cambridge University Press, 1939), Vol. I, p. 486.

was a discriminatory relief of agriculture from property taxes. The beginning of a new spirit came during the 'seventies. In 1872, France denounced the Cobden Treaty of 1860. In 1879, Germany turned to higher levels of protection of agriculture; other continental countries followed in the 'eighties, but still tariffs were lower than they had been before the movement toward including most-favored-nation provisions in treaties began. In Britain questions were raised about continuing free trade with countries that increased protection. This mild reaction — the "fair-trade" movement — began in 1881 and abruptly aborted in 1886. Ironically, it was defeated by Joseph Chamberlain, the advocate, twenty years later, of Imperial Preference. Even as late as 1886, therefore, Britain's commitment to free trade remained strong.[6]

The movement to free trade was initiated by those who believed that Britain and the rest of the world would gain in welfare and that the losses would be borne by a privileged class within Britain. It was joined by others like Cobden and Bright for whom it became a religion of welfare for the working classes. In 1865, Mill wrote of "the flush of prosperity occasioned by free trade";[7] thirty-eight years later, Alfred Marshall still believed:

> It is absolutely essential — for England's hopes of retaining a high place in the world, that she should neglect no opportunity of increasing the alertness of her industrial population in general, and her manufacturers in particular; and for this purpose there is no device to be compared in efficiency with the plan of keeping her markets open to the new products of other nations, and especially to those of American inventive genius and of German systematic thought and scientific training.[8]

For a century and a quarter, Britain's leading economists advocated free trade in the interest of British welfare; for sixty years, British imports entered virtually free of tariff. Both Mill and Marshall were perfectly aware that, in the period of Britain's greatest industrial lead, some restriction of trade would have

---

[6] Nonetheless, a slight change of temper is discernible; in 1887 an act was passed that required that all imported merchandise be labeled with the country of origin.

[7] J. S. Mill, *Principles of Political Economy*, Ashley, ed. (London: Longmans, Green & Co., 1909), p. 384.

[8] Alfred Marshall, *Official Papers* (London: Macmillan & Co. Ltd., 1926), pp. 408–9.

shifted the terms of trade in Britain's favor; Mill recoiled in horror at the prospect of a country restricting trade in order to "draw to itself, at the expense of foreigners, a larger share than would else belong to it . . . the justice of expediency of destroying one of two gains, in order to engross a rather larger share of the other, does not require much discussion."[9] Mill's adherence to free trade therefore went beyond the motive of maximizing Britain's economic welfare.

ECONOMIC NATIONALISM AND FOREIGN POLICY

The interrelations of economic interest and foreign policy are too complex for short statements. But an examination of several of the leading foreign involvements of Britain in the nineteenth century does not reveal that foreign policy was dictated simply by economic interest or even by the economic interest of exporting manufacturers.

For example, although sympathy with the cause of the Confederate States was widespread in the upper classes, the cotton manufacturers, dependent on supplies of imported cotton that were virtually shut off by the North, sympathized with the North in large numbers. British neutrality during the American Civil War by no means demonstrates the independence of foreign policy from economic interest; it does, however, show that the dominant interest affected by the Civil War did not command a foreign policy favorable to its own interest.

In the Crimean situation we have another test of the operation of economic nationalism in foreign policy. Turkish power had so far declined that by 1854 France had set up a protectorate in Algiers, Egypt had come under the rule of its viceroy, and Russia annexed the northern and eastern shores of the Black Sea. British policy was hostile to the enlargement of Russian power in the Bosphorus. Leland Jenks interpreted British policy as intending to protect British markets.

> Great Britain displayed about 1840 the greatest eagerness to preserve the integrity of Turkey. She had a trade of long standing to the Levant, which was increasing as the machine-made products of Sheffield and Manchester drove those of Smyrna and Damascus from the market. With India too there was an interchange of products, the subject of centuries of

[9] J. S. Mill, *op. cit.*, pp. 919–20.

tradition. It was no British interest to see this market pass under the control of a government such as Russia, with a hostile fiscal system and which was little more advanced commercially than Turkey.[10]

Even Jenks, later, said: "Few things could be more harmful to the relative position of Great Britain in the world than the occupation of the Bosphorus by any one of the great continental powers."

Total British exports to Turkey and the Middle East in 1850 amounted only to £3.5 million out of £71.4 million, or 4.5 per cent of total British exports, or twice British exports to Russia, half her exports to India, and one-fourth her exports to the United States in the same year. To a representative of British commercial interests like John Bright, Britain's intervention in the Crimea and the interruption of normal trade with Russia were very upsetting. Bright denounced British intervention vigorously in a number of contemporary speeches.

> The Turkish Empire is falling, or has fallen, into a state of decay, and into anarchy so permanent as to have assumed a chronic character. . . .
> How are the interests of England involved in this question? . . . We are not going to fight for tariffs, or for markets for our exports. . . . With regard to trade, I can speak with some authority . . . the Russian trade is . . . at an end.[11]

Bright, in the same speech, did "not advise alliances with any nation, but I would cultivate friendship with all nations." Britain's interest in foreign relations, for Bright, was to promote trade, but Britain's interventions in foreign relations did not serve this end.

> Now [the Rock of Gibraltar] is not of the slightest advantage to any Englishman living, excepting to those who have pensions and occupations upon it; although every Government knows it, and although more than one Government has been anxious to give it up . . . I hope this Government will send my friend, Mr. Cobden, to Madrid, with an offer that Gibraltar shall be ceded to Spain, as being of no use to this country, and only embittering . . . the relations between

[10] Leland H. Jenks, *The Migration of British Capital to 1875* (New York: Alfred A. Knopf, 1927), pp. 295–96.

[11] John Bright, *Speeches on Questions of Public Policy*, J. E. Thorold Rogers, ed. (London: Macmillan & Co., Ltd., 1868), I, 444 *passim*.

Spain and England — and . . . he might obtain a commercial treaty with Spain, that would admit every English manufacture and every article of English produce into that country at a duty of not more than ten per cent.[12]

Bright's views were perhaps radical, even for the manufacturing-exporting class, but they do indicate that national economic self-interest by no means meant, to the "typical" English businessman of the 1850's and 1860's, support of the Ottoman Empire and stabilizing the Middle East.

While most of the business community, including even its manufacturing and exporting sections, may have taken Bright's position on foreign policy, it is nonetheless true that a portion of the business community whose affairs were with Turkey would have supported the British intervention in Turkish affairs. There is much evidence of cooperation by the British ambassadors with British businessmen seeking privileges and concessions in Turkey. To build railways, Western businessmen needed concessions under Turkish law to permit property titles to be created for the new companies. Ambassadors gave advice and interceded; this is not the same as saying that British foreign policy was subverted to the interests of the business community.

Nor, during the nineteenth century, was the opposite true: the business community was not subordinated to the foreign interests of the British government. In France, throughout the century, there are examples of government intervention in the Paris Bourse to prevent the issue of securities of unpopular nations. Although the number of occasions was small, access was denied to Germany, Egypt, and Italy; it is partly because of government sanction that so high a portion of the external debt of the Imperial Russian government was held in France at the time of the Revolution.

Even this degree of control over foreign lending was absent in England. Viner said:

I know of no published evidence that there was exercised in England during the pre-war period anything approaching a continuous and systematic government censorship over the flotation of foreign loan issues in British money markets. . . . A . . . well-informed English economist, however, has said that "it appears . . . to be customary for financiers to seek the

[12] *Ibid.,* I, p. 215.

support of the Foreign Office when negotiating new loans,"
and if an informal control did exist, it probably took the form
indicated by this statement of a voluntary consultation by financiers with Foreign Office officials before they definitely
undertook to underwrite foreign loans. In the midst of the Crimean War there were English subscriptions to a Russian loan,
and the British Foreign Minister felt himself helpless to prevent such aid to the enemy. This would indicate that at least at
that time the British government exercised no close control
over the London money market.[13]

If the Crimean involvement and the neutrality toward the bel-
ligerents in the American Civil War do not reveal any influence
of economic interest on British foreign policy, perhaps the intervention in the Suez does. Disraeli's bold purchase of the controlling interest in the Suez Canal Company (made without the
advice of his Cabinet or Commons) from the Sultan of Egypt was
a brilliant stroke as an investment. With the representation of so
large an interest, the British government was able to influence toll
charges, keeping their levels reasonably low. But the purchase
does not indicate either the use of finance to further foreign policy
or the opposite. While Suez had enormous strategic importance
for the defense of India, the financial influence of Britain in ownership did little to increase the already preponderant political influence of Britain over Egyptian affairs.

NATIONALISM AND THE EXPORT OF CAPITAL

For the typical economist of the mid-nineteenth century, the
export of capital served the national interest in the same way as
it was served by the export of goods.

> It is to the emigration of English capital that we have
> chiefly to look for keeping up a supply of cheap food and
> cheap materials of clothing, proportional to the increase of
> our population: thus enabling an increasing capital to find
> employment in the country, without reduction of profit, in
> producing manufactured articles with which to pay for this
> supply of raw produce. Thus, the exportation of capital is an
> agent of great efficacy in extending the field of employment

[13] Jacob Viner, "Political Aspects of International Finance," *Journal of
Business* (April, 1928). Viner quotes C. K. Hobson, *The Export of Capital*
(London: Constable & Company, 1914), p. *xxiv*.

for that which remains: and it may be said truly that, up to a certain point, the more capital we send away, the more we shall possess and be able to retain at home.[14]

It can hardly be said that British economists retained this outlook in our century. From the 1920's onward, British economists have become more and more uneasy about maintaining a free capital market; to do so made it more difficult to balance foreign payments and control the interest rate under the gold standard. Viner refers to an informal control over foreign capital issues in London exercised by the Bank of England between 1924 and November, 1925; there are other hints of informal control at other times. Nevertheless, the opinion of the Macmillan Committee in 1930 was that foreign lending should be encouraged in order to create export markets for British production. In a speech in the House of Lords in 1946, Keynes stated a new position:

> I do not see how we can hope to avoid [control over capital transfers]. It is not merely a question of curbing exchange speculations and movements of hot money, or even of avoiding flights of capital due to political motives, though all these it is necessary to control. . . . Unless the aggregate of the new investments which individuals are free to make overseas is kept within the amount which our favourable trade balance is capable of looking after, we lose control over the domestic rate of interest.[15]

A. K. Cairncross' important study of foreign investment in the nineteenth century was influenced by the growing skepticism of the 'twenties and 'thirties illustrated by the quotation from Keynes. Cairncross argued that under the conditions of the nineteenth century, up until 1914,

> . . . there was a sufficient coincidence of private profit and social gain in Britain's export of capital to prevent the government from exercising more than a minimum of control over investment . . . it was far from evident that uncontrolled investment would be equally advantageous in the future.[16]

[14] J. S. Mill, *op. cit.*, p. 739.
[15] Quoted in S. E. Harris, ed., *The New Economics* (New York: Alfred A. Knopf, 1947); see also *The Nation and Athenaeum*, October 23, 1926.
[16] A. K. Cairncross, *Home and Foreign Investment, 1870–1913* (London: Cambridge University Press, 1953), p. 235.

Foreign investment benefited Britain as long as the export of capital was coincident with the increase of exports of equipment and merchandise to the borrowing countries; the economies of scale realized in the export industries brought a national gain and a virtual monopoly to "large sections of our export industry." Cairncross found that the returns to investors from overseas investment were higher than from domestic investment, when adjusted for defaults. But the growing prosperity of the developing countries made them independent of Britain as a source of capital; this in turn decreased the fidelity of borrowers, making foreign investment more risky just as the dominance of Britain's export industries in the world market was lost.

> The likelihood that foreign investment would reduce the cost of British imports was less overwhelming, the fear that industries competing with our own would be fostered was more intense. Cheap capital for other countries and improving terms of trade and real wages were no longer synonymous. Foreign investment, it was apparent, might lower the standard of living instead of raising it.[17]

Even if it were true that foreign investment would no longer reduce the cost of British imports, it does not follow that Britain's interest would now be served by restricting foreign investment. This would depend on the alternative investment opportunities open at home. The benefit of the policy of unrestricted investment abroad in the nineteenth century has not been challenged by modern interpretation, even that which disapproves of continued foreign investment in the twentieth century. We can therefore assert that free trade in capital was a policy that served Britain's economic interest and at the same time served the interest of the rest of the world. British policy, while perhaps not altruistic, was, in the export of capital, consistent with a cosmopolitan outlook.

NATIONALISM AND EMPIRE

During the nineteenth century, Britain greatly extended her control over India, Burma, and South Africa, and eventually granted autonomy in the Commonwealth to Canada, Australia, and New Zealand. By the end of the century the independent members of the Commonwealth, while remaining loyal in most

[17] *Ibid.*, p. 234.

respects, had failed to build a united government for common defense and economic relations with other countries. No doubt, with its loose ties, the Commonwealth still performed the common task in crisis, but it disappointed many imperial hopes. Both Canada and Australia established protective tariffs on British as well as foreign goods by the late 'seventies. In Canada by 1879 these tariffs were high, varying from 15 to 30 per cent. Whatever British nationalist intentions were, the practices of the independent members of the empire would have prevented British policies from exploiting the whole empire for national benefits.

In India, originally exploited by the East India Company purely as an economic investment, we should see most clearly whatever evidence can be found of British economic nationalism in the nineteenth century. But the same liberal opinion that drove Britain to free trade broke the monopoly of the East India Company over India's trade, opening it equally to all between 1813 and 1833.

The civil servants who ruled India in the employ of the East India Company before 1858 regarded India

> not as a temporary possession, but as one which is to be maintained permanently, until the natives shall in some future age have abandoned most of their superstitions and prejudices, and become sufficiently enlightened, to frame a regular government for themselves, and to conduct and preserve it. Whenever such a time shall arrive, it will probably be best for both countries that the British control over India should be gradually withdrawn.[18]

Although the end of British control was postponed to the distant future, its purpose was to be for the benefit of the Indian people. And although the Indians were taxed to pay the cost of the British government, the revenues were not fixed to yield a profit to the British Treasury from the subjection of the Indians. With the end of the monopoly of India's trade, the British gave up the chief means of exploiting India — through the terms of trade; in fact, the Indians were permitted some tariffs on imports that provided a mild degree of protection for Indian textile manufacturing.[19]

[18] Sir Thomas Munro, quoted in Ramsay Muir, *The Making of British India, 1756–1858* (Manchester: Manchester University Press, 1915), pp. 284–5.
[19] A detailed discussion of the heavy pressure put on the Colonial Office by the Manchester Chamber of Commerce to set aside the Indian tariff, the difficult resistance of the Colonial Office, and the resulting modification of

The imperialism to which Jenks and others object is economic control by Britain — not as a monopoly exploiter, but with free, competitive terms of trade. If this can be called exploitation at all, it is surely the most liberal form of it. If we are to condemn the resulting close ties of Indian enterprise with British capital and their effects in creating a market for British capital goods in railway construction, government finance, etc., we would equally have to find British imperialism in the development of the United States and of the countries on the European continent. A comparison with French economic policy shows the British policy in India to have been quite liberal.

In the generation which followed Mill, a more authoritarian attitude toward India emerged in such figures as Strachey, Maine, and Stephen; and the preparation of Indians for self-government and equality with the British disappeared from the stated objectives of British administration. This change did not, however, bring any attempt to exploit India's economy for British advantage. The dramatic change brought in British imperial policy by the ministry of Joseph Chamberlain, a "sharp departure from the *laisser-faire* policy which had till then ruled our colonial administration,"[20] still did not contemplate a departure from free trade in goods and capital with the colonies. What is characterized as a departure from laissez-faire was the aggressive provision of "social overhead capital" in the new territories of Africa. Chamberlain wanted action in "any case which may occur in which by the judicious investment of British money those estates which belong to the British Crown may be developed for the benefit of their population and for the benefit of the greater population which is outside."[21]

Whereas Britain's political intervention in India grew as the East India Company's economic monopoly declined, in Nigeria British political intervention increased as British trading interests

the tariff appeared in the article "The Imperialism of Free Trade" by Peter Harnetty in *Economic History Review* XVIII, 2 (August, 1965); an earlier article on the same subject by J. Gallagher and Ronald Robinson appeared in the same journal in August, 1953. British policy was influenced by the cotton manufacturing interests. But that it permitted initially a tariff which would have hurt British exporters still more than the modified tariff indicates that colonial policy was not constructed simply to serve the needs of the exporters.

[20] R. C. K. Ensor, *England, 1870–1914* (London: Oxford University Press, 1936), p. 225.

[21] Joseph Chamberlain in a speech August 22, 1895, quoted in Ensor, *ibid.*

expanded their activities in the area of the Niger Delta. Yet the unfolding of events that led to the declaration of a Protectorate in 1885 was a complex mixture of economic motives advanced by interested consuls often acting independently of indifferent home governments; native political divisions that called in British gunboats to tip the balance — ultimately not to the advantage of native independence; the conflict over the suppression of the slave trade and between British merchants and native city-states protecting their monopoly as middlemen between inland producers and the foreigners. The gunboats arrived to prevent shipment of slaves. When British merchants were imprisoned by natives, the gunboats often intervened on the merchants' side. The use of force to break the native trading monopoly broke native political power. The Protectorate was finally established in rivalry to the surprise German imperialist move in the Cameroons in 1884. Britain's role in Nigerian history is hardly admirable; the strongest impulse toward British involvement was certainly the interest of British merchants.[22] Yet the Nigerian experience is compounded of elements that are too special for generalization to other areas. The British intervention, favoring British traders, was not opposed to the interest of all Nigerians — just those who had previously enjoyed trading monopolies with the inland.

CONCLUSIONS

British economic policy in the nineteenth century was nationalistic to the extent that its advocates believed it would contribute to the prosperity of the nation. But this nationalism was compatible with the welfare of the rest of the world. The speeches of Bright, Cobden, and Gladstone promised a train of universal prosperity and peace to follow from free trade. If their predictions were somewhat quixotic, it does not follow that free trade was a mistake or that it was selfishly contrived. Britain's national interest during the ascendancy of free trade, when Britain had a lead in industrial technology, would have been best served by a protectionist policy that would have made the terms of trade more favorable to Britain. At the time when Britain lost its monopoly position, it did not make economic sense for the nation to abandon free trade.

[22] See K. Onwuka Dike, *Trade and Politics in the Niger Delta, 1830–1885* (Oxford: Clarendon Press, 1956).

The more familiar view was expressed by C. J. Fuchs, a German
writer who published a study of English trade regulations in 1891.

> So long as England alone had . . . "the workshop of the
> world," the Manchester Free Trade theory and its cosmopoli-
> tanism were not incompatible with the strongly-marked Brit-
> ish national consciousness. But since England's political and
> economic hegemony has ceased . . . since her industrial
> monopoly . . . is gradually crumbling away, a revolution
> is preparing, in that country too, which will lead, not of course
> to an insular nationalism, but to an imperialism that will em-
> brace the whole British Empire.[23]

Contrary to Fuchs and many others, free trade was not a policy
that served the selfish national interest of Britain, whatever may
have been the beliefs or motives of its advocates.

The policy of free trade served to maximize Britain's exports
(and imports) and was in the special interest of the exporting
manufacturer. When this class found itself threatened by the competition of newly industrialized countries in the domestic markets
of those countries or in the markets of third countries, the retreat
to a protectionist policy would not have benefited either the exporting sector or the nation as a whole. Threatened by the loss
of exports to Commonwealth countries owing to increased competition of other countries, Britain and British exporters might
have gained from a preferential tariff system — Imperial Preference. Faced with the competition of imports into Britain from
other industrial countries, Britain would probably have lost, but
Britain's manufacturers certainly would have gained from the
imposition of tariffs on imports into Britain. But the reaction
against free trade took fifty years to create even the small degree
of protection that was enacted in 1907. Even if we restrict the
concept of economic nationalism to the small group in whose interest free trade and the reaction away from free trade can best
be rationalized, it still appears to have been weak by comparison
with the nationalism of the twentieth century.

If it is true that Britain's national interest was served by the
free export of capital during the free-trade period, it is not equally
true that a restriction of the free export of capital would have
been in the national interest later. Although the benefit from lend-

[23] Carl Johannes Fuchs, *The Trade Policy of Great Britain and Her Colonies since 1860* (London: Macmillan & Co. Ltd., 1905), xxxvii-xxxviii.

ing to foreigners became smaller, it does not follow that there would be an advantage to investing at home instead. Even if Britain's new position in the world capital market might have led automatically to a reduction of foreign lending and an increase in home investment, this does not argue that government policy should have intervened in the market to bring this restriction about.

The imperialist episodes late in the nineteenth century may have been motivated by a desire to maintain Britain's declining international economic and political position. Yet it cannot be said that British economic policy was more self-serving in the new colonies than at home — as we would expect of economic nationalism.

The attachment to free trade can, in some respects, be best explained as the interest of the manufacturing and exporting class in Britain. Even this explanation, although congenial to a cynical view of the political process, does not explain all the facts. Policies of economic nationalism in Britain in the nineteenth century, whether conceived as serving the nation as a whole or a special class within the nation, were weakly executed in fact, whatever were the intentions of the policy-makers.

4. THE ROLE OF NATIONALISM IN THE RISE AND DEVELOPMENT OF COMMUNIST CHINA

Robert F. Dernberger

This paper presents a particular case study of the impact of nationalism upon economic policy in the developing nations. I have developed this argument so as to review China's experience with regard to many of the hypotheses put forth in several of the other papers presented in this volume, but I have not attempted to apply the model presented by Harry G. Johnson to determine the economic benefits and costs of nationalism in Communist China, nor have I compared all of the nationalist economic policies Arcadius Kahan found in European history with their contemporary counterparts in China. Rather, I have borrowed selected arguments from these authors where doing so suited my purpose.

I am neither a historian nor a political scientist. Furthermore, my knowledge of the Chinese experience has been limited by the dictates of my own interests or the demands of my research in China's contemporary economy. Inasmuch as the purpose of these papers is to stimulate further research and discussion, however, the various hypotheses I advance should serve that purpose well. The tentative nature of these hypotheses should be kept in mind whenever I make generalizations about the underdeveloped nations as a whole on the basis of this limited knowledge of China's experience.

It is also important to explain at the outset my use of the word nationalism. While we all use the words nationalistic and nationalism in everyday speech with little trouble, I was somewhat perplexed by the fact that other contributors to this volume use these terms in significantly different ways. My first recourse was to seek a precise definition in a dictionary or encyclopedia, but the definitions I found in these sources were all biased by the relationship bewteen the words nationalism and nation. Quite simply, these sources imply that nationalism is the process of building a nation, a rather useless definition for our purposes, as I hope to show later. To adopt the above definition of nationalism in a discussion of the role of nationalism in the rise and development of Communist China would be meaningless, inasmuch as the same topic would be implied by the title "The Rise and Development of Communist China."

To be useful as an analytical concept, I believe that nationalism must have an either/or connotation. It must be possible to say that a policy is a nationalistic or an internationalistic policy, although allowances, of course, must always be made for various shades of gray. Therefore, I agree with Kahan that nation-building and economic development policies are not necessarily evidences of nationalism.[1] The nation is the accepted agency for the political action of the large group, whether it inhabits an isolated island like Iceland or a whole continent like Australia; and economic development is the unquestioned goal of all nations today. One hundred or more years ago, there may have been alternative forms of political-geographical organization as well as alternative goals with respect to the importance of material well-being. But with the exception of a few utopian philosophers who either look forward to a world government or back to the Garden of Eden, the underdeveloped nations of the world today are all attempting to build strong and independent nations and to foster economic development.

This common attempt to build strong nations and to foster economic development still leaves room for a wide variety of policies, and it is in this context that I have chosen my definition of nationalism. The word nationalism has always been used to imply discrimination in favor of nationals or national interests as against foreigners or the community of nations as a whole, and I feel that it is this definition which is most meaningful and useful for our purposes. More specifically, I define a nationalistic economic policy as one that stresses the creation of an independent economy, while an internationalistic economic development policy is one that relies heavily upon the gains from an international division of labor. It is important to note that both a nationalistic and an internationalistic economic development policy, as defined here, are compatible with a strong central government, nation-building, and planned economic development. In other words, the new nations do have a choice.

Following Johnson's suggestion that it is often necessary to go back to the political and social origins of a country's economic

[1] Arcadius Kahan, "Nineteenth-Century European Experience with Policies of Economic Nationalism," chapter 2, above.

policy in order to understand that policy,[2] I shall start my analysis
of contemporary China with a description and analysis of what
has come to be called the Chinese Revolution. In the first section
of this paper, I attempt to identify that Revolution and other revolutions in the underdeveloped nations with a struggle between
the forces of nationalism and internationalism. It is further argued
that in China, as well as in many other underdeveloped nations,
this struggle between the forces of nationalism and internationalism became a fundamental aspect of the struggle for power between the nationalistic party — appropriately named the Nationalist party in China but with various names in other underdeveloped
countries — and the Communist party. In the second part of this
paper, it is determined that the distinction between the forces of
nationalism and internationalism becomes obscured once the
struggle for power is decided, and the successful party turns its
attention to the problems of political and economic development.
An examination of the Chinese case shows that, once in power,
the Chinese Communists have adopted extremely nationalistic
economic policies. The evidence further suggests that historical
circumstances and the demands of nation-building have been responsible for these nationalistic policies.

THE CHINESE REVOLUTION: NATIONALISM
VERSUS COMMUNISM

In his perceptive analysis of political parties in a democracy,
Anthony Downs argues that a political party is in the business of
exchanging government services for power and material benefits.[3]
The major problems that the party faces are its own lack of knowledge, the costs of acquiring information, and the need to gain the
support of an ignorant electorate — ignorant either because they
do not have the ability to understand the many complex problems
facing the government or because they do not care to spend the
time necessary to understand. Therefore, political parties tend to
rely on a symbolic ideology which is easily understood — easily
understood by the members of the party as well as the electorate.
Johnson argues that in the case of the underdeveloped countries,

[2] Harry G. Johnson, "The Ideology of Economic Policy in the New States,"
chapter 8, below.
[3] Anthony Downs, "An Economic Theory of Politics in a Democracy,"
Journal of Political Economy, LXVI (April, 1957), pp. 135–50.

with both an underdeveloped democratic system and an under-developed economy, nationalism is a preclusive kind of ideology which ensures one-party government and that this factor is an important part of the tendency of the new states to establish one-party governments.[4] I believe there is a good deal of truth in this analysis of political developments in the new states. An examination of the history of modern China, however, indicates that Communism, an internationalist ideology, is an equally effective alternative ideology in the establishment of one-party government.[5]

The Chinese Revolution has passed through three discrete phases: a traditional-reform, a revolutionary-nationalist, and now a Communist phase.[6] During the traditional-reform period, beginning in the mid-nineteenth century and lasting until the beginning of the twentieth century, the Chinese were forced to reassess their traditional values under overwhelming outside pressure from the West. As long as trade between China and the West had been carried out on a limited scale at the port of Canton — the only Chinese port open to trade — it was possible for the Chinese to view this trade as an extension of their historical tribute relations with the barbarians. When the British East India Company lost its monopoly of the China trade in 1834, however, private merchants, who were not so accommodating as officials of the company, were absorbed by the illusion of a huge Chinese market and incensed at the restrictions placed on the trade by the Chinese government.

The downfall of imperial China, bringing with it a serious weakening of the Chinese traditional value system, was assured when these private merchants were successful in their appeal to

[4] Johnson, "A Theoretical Model of Economic Nationalism in New and Developing States," chapter 1, above.

[5] The objection may be made that Communism, as an ideology, is utilized by nationalists to gain political power. As the concluding section of this paper will show, the activities and policies of the Communists, once they gain power, tend to support this objection. Nonetheless, I do not believe this objection invalidates the argument that Communism, as an ideology, is an internationalist ideology.

[6] See John King Fairbank, *The United States and China* (New York: Viking Press, 1962), especially Chapter 9, "The Revolutionary Process: Reform and Revolution," Chapter 10, "The Rise of the Kuomintang"; and Chapter 13, "The Rise of the Communist Party." This work also has a useful annotated bibliography for the following discussion of Chinese history between 1840 and the present.

E

their home governments for military support. Actually, the merchants appealed to the home textile manufacturers, who in turn appealed to the home government; but the home government, once involved, was more concerned with forcing China to recognize the equality of the nation-states than in enforcing the rights and privileges of private merchants. Following the Opium War in 1840, the concessions granted by the Treaty of Nanking enabled the private merchants to prove for themselves that the huge Chinese market did not exist. Opium imports into China increased immediately after 1840, but the domestic authority of the Chinese government was seriously weakened by the continued wars between China and the Western powers during the last half of the nineteenth century; the domestic production of opium soon ended this rapid growth in opium imports.

It was not until after the turn of the century, when the Chinese accepted kerosene as a cheap and efficient source of light and heat, that the Westerners found a commodity with a widespread and growing Chinese market. In brief, the private merchants had been successful in securing the concessions they had sought, only to be disillusioned by the small actual size of the Chinese market;[7] but the European powers continued to wage and win wars with the Chinese.

Despite the provisions of the treaties that were signed after each Western defeat of China, the Chinese refused to abandon the imperial system. The Chinese Emperor was considered as the direct link between heaven and mankind — not just the Chinese, but all mankind. There was only one civilization: the Chinese. China had been invaded by barbarians before, but these invaders had sooner or later either adopted Chinese civilization as their own or had eventually been defeated by the Chinese. Many Chinese reformers in the last half of the nineteenth century were advocating the creation of a modern army and its necessary industrial base or the creation of a modern educational system, but none of those reformers seriously questioned traditional Chinese institutions or the Chinese value system — none, that is, until China was defeated by an Asian power, Japan, in the 1890's.

To the Chinese, Japan was a prime example of a barbarian country on the fringes of the Chinese civilization. Japan had

[7] There has been a recent revival in the West of belief in the prospect of an unlimited market in China.

adopted Chinese institutions and values, had even borrowed the Chinese written language, and had also sent tribute to China in the past. Shortly after adopting Western institutions, however, Japan had easily defeated China in the Sino-Japanese War, a defeat that shook the self-confidence of the Westerners as well as the confidence of the Chinese. Several Chinese, including Sun Yat-sen, thought that the answer was simple: nationalism and democracy.

To Sun Yat-sen the reason for the strength of the Western nations and Japan after 1860, and the reason that they had so quickly bypassed the imperial power of the Chinese Empire, was that all of them had abandoned their traditional political system for democracy and in doing so had been motivated by a strong sense of nationalism. Sun Yat-sen was never a man to be worried about either logic or the facts. According to him, the Chinese people were like a "rope of sand," and the cosmopolitan Chinese had been unable to cope with these new forces of nationalism. Only the incessant struggle between the Western nation-states themselves over the division of the Chinese melon had prevented China from becoming a colony. Sun's mission was as simple as his analysis: he called for the formation of a revolutionary nationalist party, the overthrow of the imperial government, and the establishment of a democracy.

Even though the Chinese were ruled by a foreign dynasty — the Manchus — at the time, Sun Yat-sen still encountered great difficulty in making nationalists out of the Chinese.[8] His greatest support came from the Chinese living in foreign countries. The Revolution of 1911 was successful not because there was a ground swell of nationalist sentiment or because there was a great desire for democracy on the part of the Chinese, but because there was strong support for the Revolution from traditional Confucian political and military provincial authorities. In 1911 these provincial authorities were engaged in a "states-rights" argument with the

[8] It may be argued that the Chinese had always felt a strong sense of ethnic or cultural nationalism in their common racial and cultural identity and history. However, this ethnic or cultural nationalism was not restricted to a given geographical area or nation, nor did the Chinese conceive of their government's authority as limited to that area. While the reference has been greatly overworked, it is true that the very word for China in the Chinese language is the "central kingdom," which contradicts the idea of a nation-state among equals.

central government about jurisdiction over as-yet-unbuilt railroads. Once the Revolution was successful, however, the Nationalist party set out to gain control of the government. It took them almost twenty years, but by 1927–28, the central government of China was in the hands of the Nationalist party and its new leader, Chiang Kai-shek. Democracy, of course, had been destroyed, to remain only as a long-run goal. In the late 1920's the immediate task of the Nationalist party became that of justifying its one-party rule through a strong appeal to nationalism.

Nationalism, however, was still an alien idea to the Chinese. In effect, the Nationalists were attempting to skip the first two stages in the development of nationalism described by Kruger[9] and to proceed immediately to the third stage. In that stage, the government no longer draws upon the existing nationalist sentiment which is held by the nationals of the nation; instead the nationalistic symbols are created by the government of the nation itself.

A more extensive investigation of this important characteristic of Chinese nationalism would exceed the purposes of this paper; I will refer to only two aspects of the Nationalist party's program. First, it became a matter of official doctrine that Western religion, institutions, social science theories, literature, and in fact almost every aspect of Western civilization, were not applicable to China. China was different from all other nations. Chiang Kai-shek even went so far as to publish a study, *Chinese Economic Theory*, in which it was argued that Western economic theory was applicable to the Western economies and that, inasmuch as China had different economic institutions, the Chinese needed a different theory.[10]

This doctrine was strikingly illustrated during World War II. At that time, many responsible fiscal and monetary authorities

[9] In an unpublished paper presented to a seminar of the Committee, Leonard Kruger summarized the development of nationalism in Europe into four stages: (1) national consciousness; (2) the use of nationalism as the framework to rationalize and realize universal ideals; (3) the nationalization of universal ideals and the creation of national ideals; and (4) the development of nationalism itself into an international principle.

[10] An English translation can be found in Chiang Kai-shek, *China's Destiny* (New York: Ray Publishers, 1947), pp. 239–92. Chiang does not confine his argument to China's need for a different theory. He prophesies that after World War II Westerners "will abandon their selfish individualism and materialism [and] . . . will strive to attain the same goal as that prescribed in the economic theories of ancient China" (p. 263).

who had been trained in the West tried in vain to cut the budget deficit and to stop the rapid increase in the stock of money which was causing the rampant inflation. They were rebuffed and told that their arguments rested upon Western economic theories and were therefore not applicable to the situation in China.[11]

Second, the Nationalists argued that most of China's ills were the responsibility of the West. According to the Nationalists, the Chinese eventually would have modernized both their government and their economy, but the West and Japan had used military force to violate China's sovereignty for selfish ends. Therefore, China's first and foremost task was to drive out these invaders; only then would it be possible to tackle the job of modernization.[12] Chiang's vehemence against the West, expressed in his book, *China's Destiny*, is almost as anti-Western as any Communist propaganda attack on the United States today.[13] In summary, during the 1920's and 1930's, the Nationalist party was trying to

[11] "When the Japanese attacked China, the leaders of the Nationalist government pledged that they would wage a total war against the aggressor without regard for cost or concern about the potential inflationary consequences. . . . The Chinese people wholeheartedly endorsed the sentiments of the government without any conception of the burden they would have to bear in respect to rising price levels. A few economists advocated heavier taxation and controls on consumers' spending, such as those employed by the Western nations in World War I; but their ideas were dismissed by the Ministry of Finance and the business community as academic and impractical for China. . . . On the basis of the monetary stability of the prewar years, Generalissimo Chiang Kai-shek was overconfident of his ability to surmount the financial obstacles of a war economy. . . . The government leaders were swayed by a strange combination of traditional Chinese beliefs and modern authoritarian ideas: 'where there is land, there is money,' and 'where there is absolute power, there are goods'" (Chang Chia-ao, *The Inflationary Spiral: The Experience in China, 1939–1950* [New York: John Wiley & Sons, 1958], pp. 14–15, 18). Mr. Chang was associated with the Bank of China and participated in the organization of China's modern banking system.

[12] The first sentence of Chapter Two, "The Origins of National Humiliation and Sources of the Revolution," of Chiang Kai-shek's *China's Destiny* reads as follows: "The deterioration of China's national position and the low morale of the people during the last hundred years can be largely attributed to the unequal treaties" (p. 44).

[13] According to Philip Jaffe, whose translation of Chiang's book is cited in this paper, the United States State Department refused the request of six congressmen to see the State Department's translation of *China's Destiny* in January, 1946, on the ground that "it was not a propitious moment at which to make this document public." Although the Chinese edition was published in 1943 and represented "the political philosophy of China's ruling clique [in its] vigorous denunciation of Western imperialist penetration of China" (pp. 18–19), the first English translation was not published until 1947 —

create in the Chinese people a strong nationalist feeling that would justify and solidify the Nationalist government's one-party rule.

Effective opposition to this one-party rule was provided by the Communist party, founded in 1921 by a small group of intellectuals who had learned their Marx from Lenin. As far as I know, Marx's works were not translated into Chinese until the late 1920's or early 1930's. It was Lenin's theory of imperialism — in other words, Lenin's rewriting of Marx to fit actual developments in the world since the mid-nineteenth century — that gave these intellectuals their argument against the Nationalists.[14] The Chinese Communists argued that China was no different from any other country, that like all countries it had passed from the stage of primitive communism into the stage of feudalism, and that in the 1920's it was in the stage of hyper-colonialism. The last stage gained its exquisite name because no one imperialist country had colonized China. Rather, all of them had done so and, inasmuch as they were never able to agree on how to divide the spoils, they were forced to leave a Chinese government in existence.

In their early days, the Chinese Communists called for a bourgeois-democratic revolution that would establish capitalism in China and at the same time hasten the decline of the imperialist powers. After taking part in the bourgeois-democratic revolution and the establishment of capitalism, the Communists would then seize power. The importance, from our point of view, of this Communist analysis of China's history was that it directly countered the argument of the Nationalists. Moreover, this internationalist ideology, which explained China's past in "scientific" terms with assumed worldwide validity and presented a program for the future that promised the creation of a strong China in cooperation with all nation-states, quickly gained the support of the Chinese

after the end of World War II. Jaffe's translation contains both the original and revised versions, the latter modifying slightly some of the stronger attacks on the West included in the former. It is frequently claimed that most of Chiang Kai-shek's writings were ghost-written by Tao Hsi-sheng, a Confucian scholar.

[14] For an excellent study of how Communism came to China via Lenin's theory of imperialism and how the Chinese Communists were able to replace Sun Yat-sen's analysis of imperialism with that of Lenin as a meaningful interpretation of China's historical experience, see C. F. Remer, "International Economics and the Rise of Chinese Communism," in *Three Essays on the International Economics of Communist China* (Ann Arbor: University of Michigan Press, 1959).

intelligentsia, the leadership class in China for almost twenty centuries. The first great conflict between the Communist and the Nationalist ideologies — often overlooked by Western observers — ended in victory for the Communists and played an important part in the transfer of the leadership of the Chinese Revolution into their hands.[15]

The second great victory of the Chinese Communists in their struggle for power was due to Mao's insistence that they should abandon the attempt to follow their ideology to the letter. The orders from Stalin were that the Chinese Communists should organize the proletariat and join with the Nationalists in the bourgeois-democratic revolution. Mao openly admitted that China had no proletariat, and to his credit he recognized that the Chinese Revolution belonged to those who would lead the peasants. Although he was removed from his party post for advocating such heresy, Mao organized the leadership for this peasant Revolution in the rural soviets he set up during the early 1930's. He eventually emerged from these soviets as the leader, not only of the peasant Revolution, but of the Chinese Revolution and of the government of mainland China as well.[16]

The above brief examination of the Chinese Revolution and my limited knowledge of similar revolutions in the underdeveloped countries of the world lead me to conclude with the following hypothesis: The fundamental struggle in the underdeveloped countries today is not a struggle between democracy and totalitarianism or between free enterprise and nationalization, but between nationalism and Communism. According to Albert Breton,[17] nationalism is a policy which redistributes income from the working

[15] "Most of the present leaders of Marxist thought in China began . . . in the period 1927–1933 as exponents of the attempt to distinguish a specifically or characteristically 'Chinese' society or culture; mostly they failed, and in the next decade turned to Marxism. . . . It is possible that few movements in China gained a greater number of effective adherents, and likely that none gained so many from among men of superior intellectual ability, as the 'Chinese History Controversy' of the 1930's, calling for a full study and reformulation of the historical 'personality' of the Chinese nation, and its social and cultural identity" (E. Stuart Kirby, *Introduction to the Economic History of China* [London: George Allen & Unwin, 1954], pp. 24–25).

[16] For an excellent analysis of Mao's rise to power in the Chinese Communist party, see Benjamin I. Schwartz, *Chinese Communism and the Rise of Mao* (Cambridge, Mass.: Harvard University Press, 1951).

[17] Albert Breton, "The Economics of Nationalism," *Journal of Political Economy*, LXXII (August, 1964): 378–79.

class to the middle class. The appeal of Communism is that it is a policy that aims at redistributing income from the upper and middle classes to the working class. Evidence suggests that this appeal of Communism is not always justified, but our purpose here is to test the hypothesis stated and not whether Communism carries out its promises in practice.

This first hypothesis can also be made the basis of a second hypothesis concerning the stability of the government that emerges from this struggle between Nationalism and Communism in the new states. In Communist movements, political leaders create and retain control over their own military and use that military to gain power and hold it. In Nationalist movements, political leaders may gain power through the ballot box but ultimately rely upon an independent military to gain and hold that power. In some cases the independent military seizes control of both the Nationalist movement and the government. In any event, both the Communists and the Nationalists aim at one-party rule. It is dangerous to draw a conclusion from such a broad characterization of the hypothesized current Nationalist-Communist struggle in the new nations. Nonetheless, the distinction made here between these movements and their source of power and the empirical evidence available would suggest that if the Communists are successful, their one-party rule tends to be more stable than Nationalist one-party rule, except in those instances where the military seizes control of the latter.

CHINESE COMMUNIST POLICY: EXPEDIENCY VERSUS DOCTRINE

To offset this advantage of superior stability, however, once the Communists succeed in gaining power, they face two problems which the Nationalists would find much easier to solve. Whichever party gains power in the underdeveloped countries, that party must devote itself to the task of nation-building. I believe there is no question but that the ideology of the Nationalist parties lends itself to this task much more than does the ideology of Communism.[18] On the other hand, the Communist revolutions

[18] The argument here is restricted to the ideologies of the two groups and does not include the relative effectiveness of their organization. The argument also makes a distinction between the ideology and strategy of the Chinese Communists. For example, during World War II, Mao did advocate a united

in the underdeveloped countries have been revolutions against colonial powers or domestic groups closely associated with colonial powers; and this anti-imperialistic or anti-colonial aspect of the Communist revolutions greatly facilitates their attempt to build a nation. This is especially true in the case of the Chinese Communists, who have utilized their anti-imperialist propaganda most successfully in unifying the Chinese behind the Communist government. To an outside observer, these rallying cries of patriotism appear to be nothing more than nationalism; but we have excluded nation-building itself from our definition of nationalism.

Once in power, the new Communist leaders face the difficult problem of transmitting their decisions to both the bureaucrats who are to put their decisions into effect and the citizens who are to obey them. Here too the ideology of the Nationalists lends itself to this task of transmitting information and securing a response much more than does the ideology of the Communist parties. Johnson's paper mentions the advantage a nationalist preclusive ideology gives to the leaders in the new states;[19] I shall outline the problems encountered by the Chinese Communists.

If a monetary value were to be placed on the published edicts and directives issued in Peking in the last thirteen years, the Chinese would have experienced the fastest rate of growth the world has ever known and their national income would rival that of the United States. Every desired action on the part of the bureaucrats — and there are approximately fifteen million of them — must be spelled out in detail. Not only is Marxism a poor guide for practical day-to-day political and economic problems, but with their emphasis on doctrinal purity, even after the decisions have been made and distributed throughout the country, the party theoreticians are still left with the job of reinterpreting Communist doctrine to justify the actions taken. The flood of detailed directives helps those carrying out research on modern China, but the need to publish detailed centralized decisions on almost every aspect of the political and economic administration of China has caused the Chinese Communists considerable trouble.

What is most important for our purposes, however, is that the Chinese Communists have increasingly succumbed to the utiliza-

---

front with the Nationalists against the Japanese invasion and attempted to appeal to the nationalistic sympathies of the Chinese people for support.

[19] Johnson, *op. cit.*

tion of nationalistic symbols and slogans to assist them in their efforts to communicate and explain the administrative decisions of the new government. In other words, the clear distinction that is made between the Nationalist and Communist ideologies during their struggle for power in the new states becomes much less precise when the victorious party must turn its attention to the building of the new nation. I believe the reason is simple, for, as Johnson has pointed out, the symbols of a preclusive Nationalist ideology, unlike the Communist ideology, serve well in achieving the latter task.

The obscuring of the fundamental distinction that has been made between nationalism and Communism becomes complete in the case of economic policy; the Communist governments adopt economic policies that are more nationalistic than those found in many new states under nationalistic governments.

The Communist preference for creating independent economies is largely the result of historical circumstances.[20] While the Communist ideology advocates an international doctrine that knows no national boundaries and asks the workers of the world — not the nation — to unite, it is the workers of only one nation — not the world — that answer the call.

The success of the Russian Revolution in 1917 gave rise to the need for a revision of the Communist doctrine in order to cope with the situation of one Communist country surrounded by a hostile capitalist world. In regard to economic policy, the principle that clearly emerged was one of self-sufficiency or autarky. This can first be seen in Lenin's stand on the question of protection for "infant industries" in the course of Russian economic development. Nikolai Bukharin felt that domestic producers could be protected adequately by a system of high tariffs. Lenin, on the other hand, argued for a state monopoly of foreign trade. "Bukharin does not see that no policy of tariffs can be effective in the imperialist epoch when there is a monstrous difference between the poor countries and those of unbelievable wealth. Bukharin refers to protection by tariffs, failing to see that under the condi-

[20] As will be noted, the following argument implicitly assumes that the Communists, once in power, intended to implement the precepts of their ideology but were prevented from doing so by historical necessity. It has already been noted that a counter-argument exists — namely, that the Communists were nothing more than Nationalists who had seized power by using the Communist ideology.

tions referred to, any one of the wealthiest countries can break down this protection."[21] Lenin was fearful of capitalists willing to suffer economic losses for the sake of flooding the Soviet market at cut prices, dominating Soviet producers, and undermining the Soviet government by weakening its economic power. The Soviet belief in economic self-sufficiency was born in a period of instability as a policy of self-defense, not as a proposition derived from fundamental theory.

The policy of autarky, however, soon became built into the Communist view of international economic relations. This may have been due in part to the action of Western countries from 1918 to 1920: Russian gold was often refused, or accepted only at reduced prices, when it was offered for goods in the West. In the 1920's, when the Russians attempted to buy machinery for industrialization with large-scale exports, mainly to Britain, Britain accused them of "dumping" and in 1927 broke off diplomatic relations.[22] In 1925, Stalin told the XIV Party Congress: "We must construct our economy in such a way that our country does not become an appendage to the world capitalist system . . . that our economy shall develop not as a subnumerary of capitalism but as an independent economic entity."[23] In 1927, during the period when some elements of capitalism were being reestablished in the domestic economy, Stalin refused to remove the state monopoly of foreign trade, repeating Lenin's argument that foreign capitalists would swamp the domestic economy with goods and weaken its economic and political position.[24]

The policy of self-sufficiency was reflected in Russia's foreign trade in the 1930's. From 1926 to 1934, the Soviet Union utilized foreign trade to import industrial equipment and machinery; such imports constituted 28 per cent of its total imports in 1929 and increased to 52.5 per cent in 1932. During the 1930's, these imports were greatly reduced as a result of the new emphasis on self-sufficiency and, by 1940, Soviet trade was balanced and at a

---

[21] V. I. Lenin, *Sochineniia* (*Collected Works*), XXVII, 3d ed., 1927–28, p. 381. Quoted from John Hazard, "State Teaching in History and Theory," *Law and Contemporary Problems* (Spring, 1959), p. 245.

[22] V. Katkoff, *Soviet Economy, 1940–1965* (Baltimore: Dangary Publishing Co., 1961), p. 432.

[23] Quoted from Robert L. Allen, *Soviet Economic Warfare* (Washington, D.C.: Public Affairs Press, 1960), p. 58.

[24] Hazard, *op. cit.*, p. 246.

low level.[25] What is of interest is that the policy of autarky was no longer motivated by the necessity of self-defense; the Soviet Union had already experienced trade with the West and had obtained valuable industrial equipment and machinery, but Stalin continued to follow a program of self-sufficiency by choice.

The same argument of historical circumstances can be applied to the development of bilateral trade agreements in the foreign trade of Communist countries. Although the Soviet state foreign trade companies were created in 1918 and operated within the framework of a foreign trade plan following the introduction of planning in 1928, these companies were able to purchase imports or sell exports in the best world markets. The direction of foreign trade was not important as long as total imports were balanced by total exports plus available foreign exchange, loans, and gold. This multilateral character of Soviet foreign trade was possible as long as foreign currencies, especially the pound sterling and the dollar, were multilaterally transferable. Inasmuch as all of the Soviet trading partners, especially the suppliers of industrial equipment, were "hostile" countries, trading with one was just as distasteful as trading with another. By trading in a multilateral manner, the Soviet Union obtained the normal benefits from the international division of labor, and there was little reason for the negotiation of bilateral trade agreements.[26] The foreign trade of the Soviet Union from 1918 to 1940 suggests that bilateral trading agreements are neither required nor necessarily beneficial to a planned economy or a system of unilateral state foreign trading.

On the other hand, those countries of Eastern Europe that at a later time, with the Soviet Union, formed the Soviet bloc were the very countries of Europe that signed the greatest number of bilateral trade and payments agreements during the 1930's. In

[25] Katkoff, op. cit., p. 432.

[26] According to Raymond Mikesell, "Russia's interwar trade was largely multilateral in character and she made relatively little effort to use her trade as a bargaining weapon for creating economic or political advantage" (Raymond Mikesell and Jack Behrmann, Financing Free World Trade with the Sino-Soviet Bloc [Princeton: Princeton University Press, 1958], p. 3). The Soviet Union negotiated three clearing agreements in 1936 and five in 1939. In 1937, only 18 per cent of Soviet imports and 9 per cent of Soviet exports were financed through these clearing agreements. This was far below the average for European countries during the same period (Margaret S. Gordon, Barriers to World Trade [New York: Macmillan, 1941] p. 131).

1936, twenty European countries had an average of 4.75 such agreements, while Bulgaria, Czechoslovakia, Hungary, Poland, and Rumania had an average of 10.4 agreements. In 1937, 25 per cent of the trade of eighteen European countries was carried out under these trade and clearing agreements, while the figure for the five Eastern European countries was approximately 50 per cent.[27] The increase in the use of bilateral trade and payments agreements in the 1930's was due to the world depression and the resulting foreign exchange and international payments problems. The reason for their relatively greater use by the nations of Eastern Europe, however, was Germany's adoption of these agreements to cover its trade relations with the Balkan states, a policy that yielded both political and economic advantages to Germany. At the end of World War II, the countries of Eastern Europe had shared an experience in their recent past of foreign trade under bilateral trade and payments agreements; while the Soviet Union, with state planning and state trading, had not adopted these agreements to any significant extent.[28]

With the creation of the Soviet bloc at the end of World War II, the Soviet Union imposed closer Soviet-satellite economic relations upon each of the countries in Eastern Europe. The policy was initially enforced by means of the large reparations assessed by the Soviet Union on each of these countries, committing a large share of satellite export capacity to trade with the Soviet Union.[29] As long as the reparations commitments continued, it was not necessary for the Soviet Union to enforce closer economic ties by means of bilateral trade and payments agreements. The immediate postwar Soviet-satellite trade did not appear to be of a permanent nature, however, and Soviet trade with several of the satellite countries in Eastern Europe was a smaller share of the latter's total trade in 1947 than it had been in 1946. At the same time the European satellites were invited to increase their participation in

[27] Gordon, *op. cit.*, pp. 130–31, 133.

[28] The difference in experience was not entirely due to government policy, inasmuch as the Soviet Union had already adopted measures to isolate the Soviet economy from the influence of world markets; the smaller countries of Eastern Europe were still integrated into the world economy and were subject to the interwar currency and payments difficulties.

[29] Closer Soviet-satellite economic ties were also reinforced by the creation of Soviet-satellite joint stock companies, partly in the nature of seized German property. See Harry Schwartz, *Russia's Soviet Economy* (Englewood Cliffs: Prentice-Hall, 1958 [2d ed.]), p. 600.

trade with the non-Communist countries by joining such international organizations as the World Bank, the International Monetary Fund, and the Food and Agricultural Organization and participating in the Marshall Plan. Faced with the threat of losing control over the international economic relations of the satellite countries, the Soviet Union sought to enforce the maximum dependence of the satellites upon the Soviet economy. The satellites were not allowed to participate in the above international organizations, and the attempt was made to create an intra-bloc market.[30] Bilateral trade agreements played an important role in this attempt and all of the Soviet-satellite and intra-satellite trade was carried out within bilateral trade agreements.

The emergence of the Soviet bloc also called for another revision in Communist doctrine regarding international economic relations. Despite Soviet emphasis on autarky or self-sufficiency, international trade among the countries of the bloc was obviously necessary if these countries were to maintain viable economies. While strict autarky was no longer possible, the official policy was merely changed so that "the advantages of economic isolation came to encompass the Communist bloc as a unit."[31] According to Stalin's *Economic Problems of Socialism in the U.S.S.R.*, the goal of the Communist camp was to look forward to the day when the Communist nations would be in no need of imports from capitalistic countries.

These bilateral trade and payments agreements were not solely a device to assure Soviet control over the foreign trade of the satellite countries. With the attempt to create a separate "world market" and with the introduction of foreign trade monopolies in all of the satellite countries by 1949, these agreements became the natural results of annual negotiations between bilateral foreign trade monopolies. Despite the superior bargaining position of the Soviet Union in these negotiations, it was still necessary to settle the commodities and the quantities of them to be traded, the price at which they were to be traded, and the whole framework of commercial law that was to govern the trade. Furthermore, since the

[30] The creation of a separate and independent Soviet-bloc market was not only the result of the Soviet policy of economic isolation from the West, but was reinforced by the institution of a non-Communist embargo on shipments of "strategic" goods to these countries.

[31] Joseph S. Berliner, *Soviet Economic Aid* (New York: Frederick A. Praeger, 1958), p. 9.

ruble was not an international currency, it was also necessary to create a system of bilateral payments and clearing mechanisms, not only between the Soviet Union and the satellites, but among the satellite countries as well. It was in these circumstances that Communist China also adopted bilateral trade agreements in her trade with the countries of the Communist bloc.

China's bilateral trade and payments agreements with the Communist countries covered the major portion of China's foreign trade during the 1950's — trade between China and other Communist countries averaged about two-thirds of China's total foreign trade.[32] Bilateral trade and payments agreements were signed with the Soviet Union, Czechoslovakia, and Poland in 1950; East Germany and Hungary in 1951; Rumania and Bulgaria in 1952; and, finally, Albania in 1955. In the Asian bloc, formal trade agreements did not govern China's trade with North Korea and North Viet Nam until 1952 because of the military nature of the trade relations with those two countries in earlier years. The trade agreement signed with Outer Mongolia for 1953 reflects the creation of formal Chinese trade relations with that country, breaking the Soviet Union's almost complete monopoly of Mongolia's foreign trade. Therefore, following the creation of the People's Republic of China, all of China's foreign trade with the countries of the Communist bloc involved the signing of an annual bilateral trade agreement or annual trade protocol under an already existing trade agreement.

Nonetheless, while there is little doubt that the Soviet Union was expected to become one of China's leading partners in trade after the Communists rose to power in China, the available evidence indicates that the Chinese Communists still sought large-scale trade ties with the non-Communist countries, whose trade in 1951 accounted for only one-third of the total. Despite the introduction of the embargo on "strategic" exports to China in many non-Communist countries and the unilateral cessation of Sino-American trade in 1951, China's exports to Western Europe increased as rapidly as did China's exports to the Soviet Union; China's exports to Southeast Asia increased by over 50 per cent in 1951. The embargo did, however, have an effect on China's imports:

[32] The trade statistics cited in this paper are from Robert F. Dernberger, "Communist China's International Trade and Capital Movements" (unpublished Ph.D. dissertation, Harvard University, 1965).

66	*Robert F. Dernberger*

China's total imports from the non-Communist countries declined, even though most of the regulations restricting trade with China were not introduced until the last half of 1951. China's imports from Southeast Asia increased by over 70 per cent in 1951, largely because of cotton from Pakistan (cotton not being on the embargo list) and rubber from Ceylon (which had not adopted the embargo). China's imports from Hong Kong also increased in 1951, but Hong Kong adopted export-import controls on the China trade in June, 1951; whereas Hong Kong's exports to China had averaged 192 million HK dollars per month in the first half of 1951, they averaged only 82 million HK dollars in the last half.

The impact of the embargo on China's trade with non-Communist countries can be seen in the development of that trade following the relaxation on the embargo restrictions, especially those on metals and machinery, in 1955 and thereafter. While China's exports to Western Europe increased by 42 per cent between 1955 and 1958, China's imports from that area increased more than fourfold over the same period. Imports of metals, machinery and equipment accounted for most of this rapid increase. As a result, the export surplus China had maintained in trade with Western Europe from 1950 to 1955 became an import surplus of approximately 30 million U.S. dollars in 1957 and increased to 270 million U.S. dollars in 1958.

What is important for the discussion here is that the major portion of China's trade with the non-Communist countries was not carried out under bilateral trade and payments agreements. China signed several trade agreements with private businessmen from the West following the Moscow International Economic Conference in 1952, in an attempt to break the embargo, but this attempt failed and the agreements were not renewed. Several inter-governmental agreements have been signed with underdeveloped countries of Southeast Asia, the Near East, and Africa,[33] but these agreements have been more important for their political implications than for the amount of trade involved. In 1958, when China signed fourteen inter-government trade agreements with non-Communist countries — the largest number for any single year during the 1950's — these agreements covered only 14 per cent of China's total trade with the non-Communist world. Bilateral trade

[33] Burma, Cambodia, Ceylon, India, Indonesia, Pakistan, Afghanistan, Egypt, Guinea, Iraq, Morocco, Sudan, Syria, Tunisia.

and payments agreements were a prerequisite for China's trade with Communist countries, but China was able to trade with the non-Communist countries in the absence of such agreements. Despite this distinction, China made every effort to increase her trade ties with the non-Communist countries, the greatest increases taking place with countries (Hong Kong and Western Europe) with which China did not have bilateral trade and payments agreements.

After 1960, following the domestic agricultural crises, China's trade with the Communist countries declined and imports of food grain from the non-Communist countries increased very rapidly. These imports of food grains came mainly from Australia and Canada, neither of which countries had a trade agreement with China.

The argument of practical expediency, as against the argument of doctrinal inconsistency or duplicity, can be made for the adoption of state foreign trading companies. In 1949, even though foreign trade was a state monopoly in the Soviet bloc, the Chinese Communists allowed private foreign trade to remain, while controlling the foreign trade of China through rigid import, export, and foreign exchange controls. Private foreign trade, however, soon proved to be an obstacle to changes in trade desired by the Chinese Communist government. First, with limited foreign exchange available, the policy of government control of private trade succeeded in its attempt to balance exports and imports, but this was not the sole aim of that policy. The whole framework of import, export, and foreign exchange controls was devised so that such a balance was necessary. The main purpose of utilizing foreign trade during this period was, however, directed to securing necessary import goods, i.e., those commodities deemed necessary by the government. Trade and exchange controls helped to achieve this aim, but state foreign trading companies were required to fill the gap. On the export side, the desire was to maximize export earnings. The government soon discovered that state foreign trading companies, which could operate on a take-it-or-leave-it basis, were more successful in maximizing prices and revenues than the individual and competitive private foreign traders.[34]

[34] The Communists also quickly realized that as soon as certain items "were brought under state monopoly, then price rose on the foreign market." *Jen-nin jih-pao* (*People's Daily*), August 9, 1950.

F

Second, the Chinese Communists had made it clear in their statements before October, 1949, that the Soviet Union and the countries of the Communist bloc were to become important trading partners of China. It was possible to check trade with the West, especially with the United States, by means of export and import licensing, but it was difficult to force private traders to change from their traditional markets in the West to trading with the Communist bloc.[35] Any policy seeking to change the dominant direction of China's foreign trade would require a concomitant increase in the role of state trading.

Finally, because the inflation had contributed to the collapse of the Nationalists, the Chinese Communists launched an all-out assault on that inflation at the beginning of 1950. Government expenditures and revenues were to be centralized and revenues increased. In addition, the budget deficit in 1950 projected in the draft budget was to be reduced to 18.7 per cent of total expenditures and was to be partially offset by sales of government bonds.[36]

In January, 1950, a cash control program was introduced in the Northeast Administrative Area that required all state organs and enterprises to deposit all cash, except for minimum daily requirements, with the Northeast Bank and to make all financial transactions through the Bank. The Bank was also given control over all short-term credit; the Ministry of Finance was to regulate all loans for long-term investments.[37]

At the National Urban Supply Conference held in February, 1950, Yeh Chi-chuang, the Minister of Trade (who later became Minister of Foreign Trade), announced that twelve national trading companies were to be set up with branches in every province. The purpose of this Conference was to draft plans for the realloca-

[35] In 1949, only 8 per cent of China's foreign trade was with the Communist countries. Ch'en Chi-shih and Lin Pai-wu, *Textbook on Foreign Trade Statistics* (in Chinese) (Peking: Finance and Economics Publishers, 1958), p. 182.

[36] The deficit was to be financed 38.4 per cent by the issue of bonds and 61.1 per cent by the issue of paper money and over drafts on the People's Bank of China. Po I-po, "Report on the Draft Budget of Fiscal Revenue and Expenditures for 1950," *Hsin-hua Yüeh-pao* (*New China Monthly*) I, No. 3 (January, 1950), 650–51.

[37] In February, a National Monetary Conference advocated the adoption of this program throughout all China, and this was implemented in the Decision Concerning the Implementation of Cash Control in State Organs, issued by the Government Administrative Council on April 27, 1950. A copy of this decision can be found in *Hsin-hua Yüeh-pao*, Vol. II, No. 1 (May, 1950), 128.

tion of supply and the adjustment of prices, especially the relative prices of cotton, yarn, cloth, and grain. On March 10, 1950, the Decision on the Procedures Governing the Unification of State Trading throughout the Country created twelve nation-wide, state trading monopolies. Six of these were to control domestic trade in foodstuffs; raw cotton, cotton yarn, and cloth; sundry goods; salt; building materials for coal mining; and native products. The six others were to control the foreign trade in bristles, native products, oils and fats, tea, mineral products and imports for state enterprise.[38] The same directive assigned to the Ministry of Trade: (1) supervision of all trade performed by the state co-operative agencies, which would comprise the bulk of domestic and foreign trade when the state trading companies had fully assumed the duties assigned to them; (2) supervision of the production plans and operations of state enterprises; (3) determination of wholesale prices at major markets for commodities under the control of the state trading companies; and (4) regulation of private enterprise. By the end of 1952, the state foreign trading companies had grown to the point where they completely dominated China's foreign trade. Nonetheless, it can be seen from the above that the adoption of the policy of state foreign trading was an integral part of the over-all policy to centralize control over production, supply, and prices in an attempt to cope with the inflation.

Additional evidence of the resort to expediency rather than doctrine in the adoption of nationalistic economic policies may be found in the Chinese Communists' attitude toward the nationalization of industry. Contrary to a widely held view, the Chinese Communists have not nationalized outright either Chinese- or foreign-owned private industry. Assets owned by United States citizens were seized in retaliation for the freezing of Chinese assets in the United States. Some British companies were seized in retaliation for the decision of the House of Lords to turn over the property of the China National Aviation Corporation held in Hong Kong to the Chinese government in Taiwan, reversing the decision of the Hong Kong Court. In general, while subject to heavy taxation

[38] The text of this decision can be found in *Concordance of Fiscal and Economic Policies and Ordinances of the Central People's Government*, compiled by the Finance and Economic Commission of the Government Administration Council, Vol. II: 403–7.

and high wage demands from Communist-dominated unions, private and foreign firms were allowed to remain in business. The foreign firms ultimately abandoned their operations in China, often turning their assets over to the Chinese Communists in payment of delinquent taxes and wages. The private firms, after continual harassment from the government in the early 1950's, took advantage of the opportunity to become joint state-private enterprises during the collectivization movement in 1956.

Planning was, of course, an article of faith to Chinese Communism, and an annual national economic plan was announced for 1953. Planning was, however, believed to be an essential method for obtaining economic development in China, and I have ruled out the general desire for economic development as evidence of a nationalistic economic policy. Furthermore, bilateral trade and payments agreements, state foreign trade monopolies, and nationalized industries are not necessary conditions for effective economic planning. It was hypothesized in an earlier section of the discussion that nationalistic economic policies — that is, bilateral trade and payments agreements, state foreign trade monopolies, and nationalized industries — are not a necessary corollary of ideological Communism as the representative of an internationalistic ideology in the new nations. This section of the discussion has attempted to present evidence, weak as that evidence may be, for the argument that the adoption of nationalistic economic policies by the Chinese Communists was greatly influenced by historical circumstances.

Nonetheless, on the basis of this brief examination of the economic policies adopted by the Chinese Communists following their rise to power, it would be most difficult to support the clear distinction made earlier in this paper between nationalism and Communism. Does the evidence of the new states suggest that whoever gains power in these countries — be they nationalists or Communists — are required by the overwhelming difficulties of maintaining their own power while creating a new and viable nation to adopt those policies which best facilitate that task: nationalist economic and political policies? In other words, are the dictionaries and encyclopedias right after all in defining nationalism as the process of building a nation?

5. ECONOMIC NATIONALISM IN MEXICO

Manning Nash

Mexico is an interesting case for economic development theory in general, and especially for economic development under heavy state activity or the state's aegis, and with a rabid nationalism accompanying, preceding, or correlating with its development. The crude facts about Mexico are in themselves striking. It seems to be the first Latin-American nation which is going to cross the threshold into the elect of modernity. From 1939 to 1960, its physical output of goods and services tripled; its per capita income in 1965 was above three hundred American dollars; and its goods consumption shows the dimensions of a reasonably advanced economy.

Even more striking, the men who build the dams, staff the universities, run the government, invest the funds, and manage the industries are almost exclusively Mexicans. Mexico has developed itself: the rate of growth has been about 6 per cent per annum, and population growth has been about 2.7 per cent per annum — a substantial growth year after year after year, since about 1940. The crude facts of the Mexican experience are interesting, and the heavy involvement of the government makes them excessively interesting.

The government (or public) sector currently invests about 5 per cent of the gross national product (GNP) in Mexico; and domestic private investment is about 9 per cent of GNP. That nearly matches Rostow's mythical rate for growth.

All this growth took place without any over-all investment plans or even targets. Mexican economic development never had a plan. There is a plan now. Whether or not that plan will be operative is an open question.

Economic development in Mexico is a continuing goal, and all presidents since 1940 and all governments have publicly accepted responsibility for economic development and for three other things. The next president, when inaugurated, will also make a pledge to these things: the improvement of the health, education, and physical well-being of the Mexican population is the task of the government; the provision of basic industrial overhead facilities — transport, power, etc. — is mainly the job of the government;

71

import substitution is an economic policy of very high priority and has been since 1940. So the government is the custodian of GNP in Mexico, and the custodian of the nation as well.

The government as it now operates is crucial in two ways. The fact that 5 per cent of GNP is public investment really masks the magnitude of the government's role in the economy. The government is absolutely crucial in deciding who gets short-term and long-term credits; it has the ability to encourage what it considers productive investment and to choke off what it considers non-productive investment. Any relatively large-scale Mexican entrepreneur must spend much of his time going through government channels for credits. There are, in contemporary Mexico, a pervasiveness and a vigor of governmental activity. What amazes me, as an outsider, and other observers, is the high degree of particularity and discrimination with which the financial tools are applied. They review every product, every project, every industry, and it is hard to see any general government rules for who does or does not get funds.

This paper could close at this point with a syllogism: Mexico has grown substantially; Mexico has a vigorous public sector; hence, public sectors and government intervention are not inconsistent with economic growth. Why this syllogism does not hold is obvious. The described institutions of government intervention, the channels for it, and the vigor of it, have grown up over time and have changed substantially. It is not the particular set of government activities now undertaken which is responsible per se for the growth of the Mexican economy. Institutions like the Nacional Financiera, the Conicam, and other kinds of government agencies may be the products of economic development rather than its cause. Cross-sectional analysis always faces this problem.

The economic and social history of Mexico serves as a corrective. Notoriously, economic history is a projective system and not necessarily a reality. The same sets of facts have been construed differently by other interpreters. Here I present my particular version of what happened in Mexico from 1910 to 1940. Supposedly, my version is as respectable and as scholarly and as defensible as the others; but since I am a novice in Cliometrics, numbers will be few in this particular pattern analysis of history.

The important event which underlies Mexican economic development — *the* event, if we have to pick one in its history — is the

Revolution of 1910. In 1910 the Revolution started. The Revolution ended in 1940. During this revolutionary period of thirty years there was hardly any economic growth. In the twenties and thirties there were some industrial spurts, the social and economic motive power of which is mysterious. The causes are unknown, but spectacular economic development did not come until the close of the Revolution in 1940.

The Mexican Revolution is unusual in Latin America. It is the only revolution I can think of that succeeded in dismantling a traditional social structure and reassembling a much more modern social structure. There are only two other cases of genuine revolution in Latin America, and not enough time has passed to assess the cases of Cuba and Bolivia. Every other political upheaval has been closer to a game of musical chairs and coalition shifts among existing power types without basic transformation of the social structure. The Mexican Revolution had two parts: first, a dismantling of the social structure; and second, the putting together of a much more modern social structure capable of generating the two kinds of social indexes which denote development, continual growth of GNP, and absorbing change without breaking down a consensual mechanism.

The Revolution destroyed Latin-American traditionality, which at the turn of the century had these salient features: a wealthy, aristocratic, cosmopolitan group who lived in cities but had extensive land holdings, in alliance with foreign capitalists — American, English, and some German — guided by what the Mexicans called the científicos. The científicos are best described by reference to Porforio Díaz, who was President of Mexico for longer than anyone else; they are what we in the United States would call laissez-faire economists, who went in for law, justice, peace, easy taxes, and the encouragement of foreign arts — John Stuart Mill's recipe for economic development.

These policies resulted not in progress but in the polarization of Mexican society into a wealthy cosmopolitan elite who had large land holdings and were doing very well, facing peasants, peons, Indians, and a poor urban mass who had very little social mobility. Latin-American traditionality, then, is a system of values based on this kind of cosmopolitan land-holding elite and a stratification system which is strongly polarized between the mass of the people and the small elite. The political power was held by a series of regional political blocs which ruled over peasants in small villages. In 1910 most peasants had no notion of Mexico. They lived in what is called the *patria chica*, which is occasionally still used in Jalisco, or even Guadalajara, but now in a more symbolic sense. In 1910 the limit of a peasant's world was his own region and his own cacique.

Then too there were deteriorating Indian villages which were losing land in the free market, getting more and more defensive and poor.

The Revolution in Mexico was started by members of a northern elite. It was a revolution in which one elite segment opposed other elite segments. The revolutionaries had no ideas of social transformation. Their slogan was purely political: "No Re-election and Free Suffrage." Once they had made a single crack in the Díaz regime, all the contradictions of the society were laid bare. It was a bloody revolution in many ways. It took several turns as one or another element or segment of Mexican society became dominant. First, it took an agrarian turn: land was redistributed, and the peasants were given ejido. Then, it took an anti-foreign turn: foreign holdings were all expropriated and the oil, mining, etc., put in Mexican hands. Finally, it took a pro-labor turn and tried to do something for the urban masses.

So from 1910 to 1940, two processes were going on: the dismantling of the old social order, and the building of the new. What the new social order holds sacred is what every president since 1940 has enunciated as a belief system and has often tried to implement. Out of this shared commitment since 1940 have come the stability of Mexico, its economic growth, the fact that it is a social order, and the political process which changes governments in a rather orderly manner.

All the presidents since 1940 have shared these values: economic growth, concern for the urban poor, agrarian revolution, independence from foreign investors, respect for the going system. They have not offered reforms for the current Mexican political institutions. Though the presidents seem very different from one another (consider the flamboyant Alemán and compare him with Cortinez), they have all shared these commitments.

The expression of these commitments and the social organization in which they are acted out is the PRI — the Partido Revolucionaro Institucional. It is no contradiction in Mexico to speak of revolutionary institutions, because the Revolution is an institution, and the PRI is the expression of national unity and political stability.

Data for the history of the PRI are not abundant — obviously, the most interesting things about any country are not open to social scientists, and I think we delude ourselves if we think we really get close to the most important decision-making in any national government. Hence, what follows relies on hearsay, gossip, newspaper reports, interviews, but not tape-recorded councils of the Party. The PRI as it developed was at first sectoral. When the Mexican society started to collapse — when the landed aristocracy and the cosmopolitans were stripped of political and economic power — the ancestor to the PRI organized itself by sections or sectors: the national labor sector, the agricultural sector, a government sector, and a military sector. The president, and all the congressmen, and any decision-maker, had to move by coalition among these sectors.

This structure of the PRI was regionalized and had local bosses, and the central government was fragile in the early stages. The PRI made its first important mutation in the regime of Cardenas, when the military sector was dropped. The military are irrelevant in Mexico: the generals are no longer actors on the stage. Mexico may be the only country in the world to show a decreasing military budget year after year. It is striking that the military get only 5 per cent of the national income. By the time of Cardenas, there was enough commitment to Mexico as a nation that the military were not useful. Latin-American military, you will recall, have specialized on their own people. Once in a while they fight another nation, but each military exists chiefly for the pacification of its nation's citizenry and not for the defense of its country.

In Cardenas' regime, the military were dropped and a popular sector of middle-class intellectuals was added. The PRI evolved from a series of oligarchs relying on a few critical sectors to a more broadly based party. The popular sector has become more and more important in the PRI. The government sector is the most important, and the government is the civil service, the técnicos, and the políticos who get re-elected. The PRI wins everything in Mexico. The PRI is so confident that they allow opposition parties, but an opposition party never gets anything at the national level — no cabinet posts, nothing really crucial. There is a wide consen-

sus in Mexican society that the PRI does in fact represent the national interest and does respond in the way that most people want
it to respond.

Within the PRI itself there are two very distinct kinds of persons; políticos and técnicos — politicians and staff experts. The
políticos are the decision-makers. There are no technical decision-
makers in Mexico, but the técnicos have much more power than
United States technical people would have, in that most of the
políticos know nothing about anything except politics. Mexican
politicians have no expert knowledge about monetary or fiscal
policy, about import substitution, about inflation control, about
any of the things needed to run a complicated economy. The
power of the técnicos lies in a very subtle sort of thing. They devise the only set of alternatives in implementing policies that
the políticos will ever scrutinize. There is thus some power in
the hands of the técnicos, since they tell the políticos about policy
alternatives and devise the means of execution.

As the PRI now works, its activities are not public. The debates
and the different positions the members of the PRI hold on any
important policy are not recorded in the press. The government
speaks with one voice — the voice of the president; there are no
congressional debates that are reported, so the electorate has little
feedback. The Mexican papers do not have policy discussions; this
kind of information is found in the gossip along the Calle
Moneda (where the government buildings are) from talk with
bureaucratic insiders.

On the basis of this fragmentary history, I want to make some
generalizations about the role of nationalism in Mexico as an
input in economic development.

What I understand to be Mexican nationalism was the conscious
building of a centralized political apparatus to which most people
would have loyalties not backed by bayonets — a legitimate, centralized nation-state. Along with that came the creation of a
symbol system expressing the legitimacy of this central political
apparatus. These social changes are costly operations. The point
I am making is that economic growth could not and would not
have begun in Mexico if these two prior activities, which used
nationalism as an input, had not been successful.

If the centralized political apparatus based on consensus rather than bayonets had not been built, and if the self-identification of most Mexicans as Mexicans were not made through a symbol system, Mexico would never have grown. Mexico would be like the other Latin-American countries. Their talented people would come and go with coups d'état, take up residence in other Spanish-speaking countries or in the United States, and never get settled.

Obviously, nationalism in Mexico rests upon two things. First, the Revolution is pervasive among intellectuals. Everybody in political life subscribes to the slogan and the meaning of the Revolution. The only people who do not are those on the far right, and they are of little importance and hold no offices. The revolutionary ideology is a mystique. It has a special form and language which the intellectuals share.

Second, there has been a conscious building of another kind of symbolic national identification: the conscious downgrading of European and Spanish symbols and the upgrading of Indian and mestizo symbols. In Mexico City one can see the latest product of this, the world's most expensive and finest anthropological museum. They started out with an investment of twenty million dollars. They plan to double that in the next year. Now what is a country like Mexico doing with a forty-million-dollar museum? An excessive interest in anthropology? Yes, but in combination with that there is the conscious drive of the government to build a symbol system which will extol the Mexican heritage. And I think that it is a very good investment as an input in economic development. Lesser examples of it are the replacement of the statue of Cortes by that of Cuathemoc, who was the brother of Montezuma and actually fought the Spanish. Montezuma is not so important because he did not do the fighting. In Mexico the ideal type of a person is a mestizo, a mixture of Indian and European. He is not the Indian, and he is not the European. The ideal Mexicans — winners of the beauty contests — are always "some kind of brown girl or guy." This has been consciously promoted through the school books, the newspapers, and government propaganda. The "Mexican" has been manufactured at great cost.

One thing that actually solidified Mexican identity and made the symbol system operative, I think, was the bold expropriation of all the oil in the country in 1939 by Cardenas. He did it, of course, against the advice of all the oil companies and against the advice of impartial observers. The opposition slogan that sticks in my mind was "Mexicans cannot get oil out of the ground." Cardenas' reply was: "If we cannot get it out, it will stay there. Then it will still be Mexican oil." And the nationalized oil company, although it has ups and downs, is a going concern, although probably not so economically efficient as when Shell and the other companies were running it. The difference is that it is an integral part of the Mexican economy and its funds are used for all sorts of other investments. Its personnel are also used in other kinds of ways. It successfully symbolizes the strength of the Mexican nation in holding off and confronting large foreign powers.

The symbol system had been consolidated by 1940. The Mexicans had confronted and defied foreign powers, including the United States, by 1940. They had diffused an image of Mexico, and they had created a centralized political apparatus working on a consensual basis. All of this was a prelude to economic development.

I do not want to sell short some things which are obviously crucial in the history: that is what makes economic history such a capricious business. World War II did give Mexico a particularly important opportunity, with Europe closed off, in regard to American needs. The Mexicans seized it. This favorable opportunity for the export of Mexican cotton, other agricultural products, and other things during the war accounted for the big economic spurt.

But one cannot credit the war alone, because Guatemala was faced with exactly the same economic opportunity, as were a number of other Latin-American countries. Mexico was ready to make use of the opportunity because of all these social transformations. I do not think that the social transformations could have been made without heavy expenditures and the conscious building of nationalism. Mexican nationalism is tempered by a kind of pragmatic decision-making. The nationalism is largely a symbol system which is consumed by the people, but it is not a direct intervening in the selection of economic projects or how funds will be invested. This seems to me to be the trick of the peculiar Mexican integration of a high-level revolutionary nationalism with unheroic pragmatic selection and control of economic projects — how that particular mix has come about, nobody knows. Most Americans who talk about Mexico, either as a country or as an economy, tend to misinterpret it (as I have just done, in some sense) because

it has never been obvious what the next source of Mexican economic growth will be. Whenever Mexico is studied, it looks as if
it is going to break up. Vernon's book [1] suggests that very thing,
which I think is just wrong. No matter when one studied Mexico,
it would appear obvious that it could not grow any more, according
to Vernon. Mexico always seems to have reached the limit, but
the record shows Mexicans have managed now for more than
two decades to show sustained high-level growth.

There is a persistent tension from income inequality in Mexico,
and this may get into the political sphere. Part of the relief of
this tension comes from a fair redistributive mechanism which
does not get into income statistics. There are many medical clinics
set up in areas of the cities where the discontent with income
distribution could be politically organized. New welfare centers
are often opened. In rural areas, where the income differential
is the worst, discontent is scattered and diffuse and cannot be
organized. I think that this is what has kept it down so far. How
long that can continue is uncertain.

The question of who has gained from the economic development
is a debate about which one reads in all Mexican economic
documents. It is fairly obvious that most workers and peasants
have not gained much. The middle class and the businesses have
gained tremendously. The reason that the workers and peasants
can be deprived of the economic gains is that they are given
psychic income and symbolic pride. Per capita income may be
three hundred dollars a year, but an income distribution scale
would show a different picture.

The cities are richer. This is one of the country's problems.
Everything is richer around Mexico City, which is like a giant
octopus taking the wealth of the country and organizing it. The
Valley of Mexico has most of the people, most of the wealth, most
of the goods, most of the income.

Nationalism seems to help keep the political process out of the
way of the economic. This is done at great expense in terms of
efficiency, but it is still important. The basis of the revolution
here is very important and not open to every country, particularly
those liberated from a colonial power. In Mexico, before real development, the land was being redistributed. This has done two

[1] Raymond Vernon (ed.), *Public Policy and Private Enterprise in Mexico*
(Cambridge: Harvard University Press, 1964).

main things. First, it has given the peasants a concrete stake in the government — it has tied many of them to a place and made them loyal PRI supporters. Second, it has allowed the government to make all its agricultural investment in modern agriculture, doing almost nothing with traditional agriculture. The peasants got a subsistence plot. That part of the agriculture has hardly grown. Any economist could demonstrate that the agrarian reform program has cut down productivity almost everywhere. But it has kept the peasants from rejecting the elite and allowed the latter to build modern irrigation dams to serve the social type "farmer" (not peasant).

The agrarian lesson of Mexico is not simple; non-Mexican Latin-American land reformers often misread Mexican experience. They talk about land reform, and they want to modernize that particular reformed agriculture. I think that the Mexicans have done it right. They redistributed the land and left it alone. They have modernized in regions fully in the commercial sectors of large-scale agriculture.

If agrarian reform and modernization are phased right and the industries and cities are expanding, the peasants who are really rotting at the bottom of the social and economic scales may leave their ejido. Ejidos kept peasants tied down for a decade or two, satisfied their immediate needs, and helped disband armies. Here again there have been gradients. Peasants have tended to move off the farms more rapidly the closer they were to areas where alternatives were open to them.

Wilbert Moore's study, *Industrialization and Labor,*[2] pins down this process of push and pull off the land. Around Puebla there were some new industries. The recruits to labor were the poorest members of traditional agriculture. They were the ones who came, stayed, became committed. And so they left the land behind. This confirms my own naïve reflection, anthropological rather than economic, that it is almost impossible to transform a dense traditional agriculture in any significant way. It is easier to start with modern agriculture. The task of getting extension services to one Indian farmer after another, and getting him to modernize, seems to be beyond the capacity of humanity. It is

[2] Wilbert E. Moore, *Industrialization and Labor* (Ithaca: Cornell University and New School for Social Research, 1951).

possible, however, that the rapid rate of agricultural innovation may invalidate this contention.

Taking Latin America as a whole and dividing it into three main components, I think that this kind of model fits only Indian Latin America — that is, Mexico, Guatemala, Peru, Bolivia, and Ecuador: the Indian republics. Then there is a part called mestizo America, and one called Euro-America. Perhaps three countries are Euro-American, and they have very different problems. They are not, as Mexico was in 1910, in any way that I can see really underdeveloped countries. Rather, they are "pathological modern." They have good economies, with good road networks, high literacy, and tremendous spurts of growth. But they have a poisoned political process. However, they do not need to build institutions.

The major point is rather obvious. A country building up a symbol system to underwrite a more or less conscious campaign of economic nationalism needs a few incidents in its past to elaborate the collective representations necessary to infuse some sense of confidence into both the elite and the peasantry for the tasks of modernization. Mexico was fortunate in having, in fact, a spectacular indigenous heritage.

The symbol system of the Revolution and the granting of ejido have kept the peasant districts from becoming hotbeds of agrarian unrest, while the process of economic development has transferred most of the gains from higher income to the middle and upper classes.

Mexico's development has been aided by the fortuitous facts of geographical location. Fortunately, it is located next to the most prosperous nation in the world. The prosperity of the United States has many direct and indirect effects on Mexican growth. Two important by-products of the migration of a half-million or so Mexicans to the United States for longer or shorter periods have been the income earned by braceros and the vocational training that some Mexicans get. Further, tourism, chiefly from the United States, is the second largest earner of foreign exchange in contemporary Mexico. And a final aspect of locality lies in the military strength of the United States, which stands as an unspoken but guaranteed defense of Mexico against international aggression. Another less tangible aspect of the United States' presence is that part of Mexican nationalism has crystallized as anti-Americanism.

The anti-Americanism does not get involved in economic policy-making, but serves to hold a good part of the intellectuals in a common confrontation. It also elevates a Mexican style of life, and destiny, as something apart from the United States style and values. This probably is a factor in accounting for the overwhelming rate of return of Mexicans to Mexico after they have come to the United States for higher education. Certainly the ability of the growing Mexican economy to absorb and utilize those trained abroad also accounts for the high rate of repatriation of foreign-trained university students.

The general contention made in this paper is simple and stark: a thirty-year period following the beginning of the Mexican Revolution was devoted chiefly to the symbolic definition of the nation and the spread of a revolutionary mythology encompassing the intellectuals and the peasantry. On this basis, the less heroic tasks of economic development and modernization could be undertaken by a pragmatic bureaucracy in combination with a business class, and the traditional peasantry rerouted from discontent and political ferment through small land grants and minor increments in level of living. This mystique is now beginning to wear thin and political and social unrest is more manifest, but the mystique accomplished the social and economic transformation; whatever unrest now erupts, it will be the unrest of a people in a modern, working nation-state.

How applicable theoretically and procedurally is the Mexican form of economic nationalism, or social transformation, to the rest of Latin America or to the other less developed countries? A view of the Mexican assets before the Revolution may in part provide some clues. In the first place, Mexico did have for more than three hundred years overarching institutions. The Catholic Church, however local and parochial it became after the decay of New Spain, never lost its claims and character as a universal and international organization. It helped lay down attitudes of submission to indivisible and remote authority. And from time to time the central state of Mexico moved into the daily lives of even the most remote Indian groups. In short, the colonial experience and the republican periods left behind supra-local political and symbolic systems which the Revolution could transform. Mexico did not begin from scratch, as compared with some of the new nations of Africa and Asia.

Furthermore, under the científicos much of what is currently called infra-structure was created — railroads, industry, market structures, and a small entrepreneurial community. Hence the Revolution had large assets to work with, and its task was transformation as much as it was sheer innovation or radical novelty.

In conclusion, I want to hazard some generalizations. Some of the propositions are tied directly into my reading of the Mexican experience, and some transcend that to point to analogues in other new nations.

First, nationalism in the Mexican context played a motivational role akin to that which the Protestant ethic is alleged to have played in the development of the Atlantic community. It energized and gave purpose to the strivings of large numbers of Mexicans, and at the same time allowed them to forego immediate returns in favor of the larger end of *Mexicanidad*. This nationalism affected the ordinary making of economic decisions; although for a long period it distorted the character of Mexican growth, it transformed the social structure and value system so that, when really significant economic opportunity arose, Mexico was able to grasp it. In the flow of history, the rabid nationalism came with the least economic opportunity, and the most pragmatic nationalism came with the greatest economic alternatives. Such fortuitous circumstances are beyond the reach of planners and the exhortations of Manchester economists, and remind us again how much of the process of economic development and modernization is tied to a particular historical trajectory, to a particular cultural heritage, to a time and space continuum that is what it is, and not to a model with parameters made by assumption or created from theory.

Lest this be misconstrued as a plea for the abandonment of nomothetic propositions about economic nationalism or modernization, I shall offer some general (and I hope non-vacuous) assertions. Economic nationalism may be a necessary input for economic development, and what superficially by the rules of immediate optimal allocation appears counter-productive may be the best investments that a developing nation can make. An investment in monuments, in symbols, in national mythology, if successful in motivating persons to strive for economic ends and to forego consumption, is an important investment in human

G

beings. By extension of a currently fashionable phrase, it may be a kind of "human capital" formation, the returns from which take a generation to materialize.

The special conditions under which a policy of economic nationalism is not self-destructive are not clear, and the ingenuity of nascent elites is required to steer a proper course. What the experience of Mexico does underwrite, generally, is that there exist different species of poverty, different varieties of traditionality, and different paths to modernity. Social scientists are faced with charting the set of linked temporal sequences against different cultural heritages in which economic nationalism is a creative rather than destructive ingredient in the process of modernization.

6. ECONOMIC NATIONALISM
IN CANADIAN POLICY

Harry G. Johnson

The evolution of Canadian economic policy since 1957 has been extremely puzzling for the outsider to understand. In the immediate postwar period, the Canadian economy became increasingly closely integrated with the United States economy in two major ways: first, through the large-scale investment of American capital in Canadian resources for export to the United States and in Canadian manufacturing; second, through the regionalizing influence of the American postwar boom and of European discrimination against dollar imports. Consequently, from 1957 on, the Canadian economy was subject to the same competitive pressures from resurgent industrial Europe as was the American. In addition to the adverse effects of the slackening of growth in the United States, Canada was also adversely affected by the tendency of American foreign investment to switch from the American continents to Europe in consequence of the European growth boom and the easing of cold war tensions.

By contrast with the United States, however, Canada was saddled with neither the responsibilities of a reserve currency country nor at that time with the obligation of maintaining a fixed exchange rate. With the freedom allowed by a floating rate, the authorities could have set out to counteract the depressive influences radiating into the Canadian economy from the semi-stagnating United States economy and the industrially competitive European countries by following an expansionary monetary policy. Such a policy—the essentials of which were well understood by Canadian economists, academic as well as governmental—would have stimulated economic activity both directly, through the influence of lower interest rates on consumption and investment, and indirectly, through the influence of lower interest rates in stemming the inflow of capital, depressing the exchange rate, and thus stimulating exports and discouraging imports.

Furthermore, on the face of the matter there were present in Canada none of the constitutional obstacles to effective policy-making that the United States administration has labored under:

An earlier version of this paper was printed in *Lloyds Bank Review*, (October, 1964) LXIV: 25–35.

the country is governed by the British Parliamentary system, with responsibility centered on the Cabinet. Moreover, the economists at the government's service, both in the various departments of the civil service and in the Bank of Canada, were of exceptionally high intellectual caliber and professional competence for a relatively small country and were accustomed to working together smoothly in the formulation and execution of economic policy.

Nevertheless, instead of the expansionary monetary policy indicated by elementary theory as appropriate to the circumstances, the policy actually adopted was one of severe monetary contraction during the crucial period 1958–60, a policy that aggravated rather than mitigated the adverse influence on the economy of external economic developments and helped to raise the unemployment rate above 7 per cent. This policy was adopted by the Governor of the Bank of Canada, it seems, partly out of an unwarranted terror of inflation and partly out of a strong conviction that it was the Governor's personal responsibility to arouse the country to the need for nationalistic economic policies. The views expressed by the Governor conformed to the nationalistic, and strongly anti-American, sentiments that had been gathering strength during the postwar boom and that had been in a substantial degree responsible for the replacement of the long-lived Liberal regime by the Conservative government headed by Mr. Diefenbaker.

The stagnation of the economy and the associated mass unemployment, aggravated by contractionary monetary policy, in turn strengthened the hands of the nationalists. It enabled them to attribute the depression of the economy to the effects on the exchange rate of the inflow of foreign (i.e., American) capital induced by the contractionary monetary policy and to argue for higher tariffs as a means of creating employment for the unemployed in Canadian secondary manufacturing industry.

At the same time, as seems generally to happen when an unsophisticated electorate is exposed to mass unemployment, there developed a general tendency to blame the unemployment, not on the over-all economic policies of the government, but on a host of special factors — inadequate education, overoptimistic investment, labor immobility, insufficiently aggressive salesmanship and incompetent business management, the shortsightedness of trade unions, and so on — and to recommend the corresponding specific remedial measures. This approach has been characteristic of the Canadian government policy ever since. Further, when the government finally got around to pursuing a deliberately expansionary fiscal and monetary policy, it was felt necessary to accompany this policy by a deliberate effort to talk down the rate of exchange to what the government considered an appropriate level.

The exchange rate ceased to be a freely floating rate and became a manipulated rate. Moreover, in the circumstances a floating rate would have floated downward fairly sharply, since it had been held up only by tight money and economic stagnation; the government consequently found itself in the position of attempting to hold the rate up rather than down. Speculation against its ability to do so eventually forced a panic decision to peg the rate, thereby throwing away the main element of freedom that the Canadian policy-makers had enjoyed by comparison with their American counterparts. But the manner in which the new pegged rate was chosen, together with the failure of the authorities to support the action by marshaling their international liquidity and the failure of the Conservative government to win a majority in the 1962 election, led to renewed speculation against the Canadian dollar, culminating in an exchange crisis.

To cope with this crisis, the government resorted to large-scale borrowing from the International Monetary Fund, Britain, and the United States; an austerity program, including cuts in government expenditure and the reintroduction of tight money; and the imposition of temporary tariff surcharges by a procedure of disputed legality. The tariff surcharges, which have subsequently been removed, fitted into a general policy of increased protectionism manifested during the period, that included tax incentives to exports and culminated in October, 1962, in the inauguration of a new and ingenious policy of export subsidization for the automotive industry, about which more will be said later.

These policy developments occurred under Diefenbaker's Conservative government and were characterized by a strongly nationalistic and anti-American flavor. The election in 1963 of a minority Liberal government headed by Lester Pearson generated the widespread expectation, both inside and outside Canada, that the country would return to the sane and internationally-minded policies that had characterized the previous Liberal regime. In fact, the new government has proved no less nationalistic and anti-American than its Conservative predecessor, and no more sophisticated in its over-all economic policies. The first budget of the Liberal Finance Minister, the Honourable Walter Gordon, reflected a strong desire to achieve a balanced budget, an objective evidently motivated mostly by the desire to command foreign confidence but clearly inappropriate to conditions of excessive unemployment. Aside from that, it contained two proposals directed at discouraging foreign (i.e., United States) direct investment in Canada: a 30 per cent tax on takeover bids for Canadian enterprises by foreigners; and an alteration of the non-resident withholding tax designed to encourage United States enterprises in Canada to sell 25 per cent of their equity to Canadians.

The first of these proposals proved to be unworkable and had to be withdrawn, while the second has since been watered down so severely as to be practically ineffective. Nevertheless, the desire to do something to curb foreign direct investment remains an active element in the government's thinking.

The budget and the government's subsequent policy also followed the Conservatives' line of treating unemployment as a series of special problems to be dealt with by specific measures — tax incentives for investment in new machinery and equipment, tax incentives for new investment in areas of heavy unemployment and unusually slow growth, tax incentives for retraining and employing older workers, and so forth — rather than as a general problem of inadequate effective demand. Subsequent budgets continued this approach. In addition, the new Liberal Minister of Industry extended the policy of subsidizing exports of automotive products introduced by the previous government. This policy was defended on grounds of increasing employment and improving the balance of payments — even though Canada has chronically run a balance-of-payments surplus, and the measure was specifically directed at increasing exports to and reducing imports from the United States, which has a serious chronic deficit. The Minister of Industry also set about recruiting a large high-level staff, whose function is to take charge of and ginger up efficiency in the various branches of Canadian manufacturing industry.

All these policies represent a continuation or intensification of the policies of the previous government; and all of them represent a peculiarly indirect approach to the pursuit of the objectives of full employment and economic growth in a country that professes economic liberalism and has been enjoying a surplus balance-of-payments position. To understand them, it is necessary to understand the general background of economic nationalism and anti-Americanism in Canada from which they spring. (I should emphasize that I refer to English-Canadian nationalism, and not to French-Canadian nationalism, which is directed against English-Canadians and not Americans.)

It is essential to realize that Canada represents the losing side of the American Revolution. The central part of the country — the Province of Ontario — was settled by embittered Tory refugees from the United States, many of whom had been deprived of their property and arrived in Canada practically destitute. The tradition of disdain for and fear of the Americans which they brought with them has had — owing to their superior education and social status — a disproportionate influence on Canadian thinking with respect to the United States ever since. Moreover, for the first part of the nineteenth century Canadians lived in fear of invasion by and absorption into the United States — they successfully withstood invasion in the War of 1812 — and it was the fear of invasion by the victorious North after the Civil War that led to the successful negotiation of the Confederation of the Canadian Provinces.

Thereafter, the new nation set itself to build a rival to the United States in the northern half of the continent, by means of Sir John A. MacDonald's "National Policy" of railway-building, protective tariffs, and immigration. In the terminology of the economic historian Hugh G. J. Aitken, the country was pursuing the two goals of political independence and economic growth, and it could combine the two by means of economic policies which directed its trade toward the European, and specifically the British, market and sought to increase its population of British origin. The policy appeared to work well in the two decades before World War I, when Canadian expansion was based on the development of wheat exports from the Western prairies, and the returning grain ships could bring loads of British immigrants — though the Canadian economic historian J. H. Dales has recently argued forcefully that this period of expansion owed little or nothing to the National Policy.[1] Be that as it may, the policy began

[1] J. H. Dales, "Some Historical and Theoretical Comment on Canada's National Policies," *Queen's Quarterly*, LXXI: x-xx, No. 3 (Autumn, 1964), pp. 297–316.

to break down in the period after World War I, when the basis
for economic development shifted to forest products and base
metals for the expanding American industrial economy, while at
the same time the flow of British immigration began to be replaced
by less easily assimilable immigrants from Central Europe.

The period of boom after World War II, which entailed increasing interdependence with the United States in the form of
increasing reliance on United States capital for the development
of Canadian resources and manufacturing and increasing dependence on the American market for exports of Canadian products
and imports of production and consumption goods, brought the
two goals of political independence of the United States and
economic growth in rivalry with the United States into open
conflict. Canada was growing faster than the United States, but
this entailed increasing economic integration with the American
economy. The greater facility of communication between the
United States and Canada, together with the flood of European
immigrants, was also steadily eroding the parochialism of the
dominant — and, in my view, anachronistic — British culture and
fostering a more cosmopolitan way of life. This development was
scornfully and inaccurately described by Canadian intellectuals
as "American cultural penetration."

On the economic side, concern over independence of the United
States concentrated on two aspects of the evolving integration of
the Canadian economy with the American: American ownership of
Canadian industry, and dependence on the United States for
imports of manufactured goods and exports of resource products.
This concern found its expression in the *Report of the Royal Commission on Canada's Economic Prospects*, set up in 1955; the Chair-
man of the Commission was Mr. Walter Gordon, then a wealthy
Toronto accountant. Without intending any disrespect to Mr. Gordon, whose conduct and ideas have consistently displayed that
sense of public responsibility that is characteristic of the best
among the owners of considerable property, it is fair to say that the
Gordon *Report's* ideas on economic policy are exactly what might
be expected of a man of his background. The *Report* combines a
recognition of the manifold benefits to Canada of American direct
investment, and the cost to the Canadian standard of living of
increased protection, with the belief that, because many "responsible" Canadians — i.e., Canadians in positions of economic

power—believe that American investment in Canada and Canadian economic interdependence with the United States are
threats to Canadian political independence, they must be genuine threats. It recommends measures to deal with these sup-
posed threats that would naturally suggest themselves either to
the chartered accountant—tax incentives to encourage Canadian
participation in management or equity ownership—or to the
responsible man of wealth and social conscience—political pressure or "ear-stroking" to persuade United States enterprises exporting Canadian resource products to perform more of the
manufacturing processes in Canada, and United States manufacturing enterprises in Canada to import fewer of their components
and manufacture more of them in Canada.

This approach to the objectives of Canadian nationalism—fiscal
incentives combined with moral suasion—was presented even
more clearly in the book *Troubled Canada* published by Gordon
after his embarkation on a political career, and it is this approach
that he sought to implement during his tenure as Minister of Finance. That tenure ended with his resignation after the election
of 1965 failed to produce the Liberal majority that he had advised
Pearson that it would. But Gordon remains a strong contender
for the succession to Pearson, and has announced his candidacy
with a new book, *A Choice for Canada: Independence or Colonial
Status*, which reiterates his worries about and proposed solutions
for the problem of American investment in Canada. Gordon's
vociferousness on this score has had the natural effect of pushing
Mitchell Sharp, now Minister of Finance and the other strong
contender for the succession, in the same direction, so that Gordon's influence is certain to be felt in future Canadian government
policy. There is good reason for thinking that the position of
American enterprise in the Canadian economy is the consequence
of the inability or unwillingness of Canadians to undertake the
massive capital commitments and entrepreneurial risks involved
in the development of Canadian natural resources and to master
the managerial and technological problems of industrial competition in the international market, and therefore for doubting the
efficacy of Gordon's proposed remedies.

The annual reports of James Coyne during his tenure as Governor of the Bank of Canada contributed to the evolution of Canadian nationalist policy ideas in several important ways. By harping

on the theme of American investment in Canada as a key element in Canada's unemployment problem and a grave threat to Canadian independence, they helped to divert Canadian attention from domestic economic, and especially monetary, policy to American investment as the prime source of aggravation of Canada's economic difficulties. Second, these pronouncements stressed and helped to give currency to the ad hoc approach to the unemployment problem; in particular, they emphasized inadequate education of the labor force and labor immobility, rather than general deficiency of demand, as the source of the trouble, thus echoing ideas which were currently being advanced in the United States as part of the contemporary defense of Republican economic policy.

Most important, Coyne's speeches did much to implant in popular Canadian economic thinking three ideas that underlie current Canadian commercial policy. The first is that Canada has a serious balance-of-payments problem because it has a current account deficit and that the deficit is attributable to an import surplus in manufactures with the United States. Yet in fact the deficit is normally matched or overmatched by a capital account surplus and serves to transfer that capital account surplus. The second idea is that the import surplus in manufactures has been the cause of unemployment in Canada. The third is that the way to cure both the balance-of-payments problem and unemployment is to reduce the import surplus in manufacturing by protective measures.

It is this set of ideas that has motivated recent Canadian policy. That policy envisaged curing both the alleged balance-of-payments problem and the actual unemployment problem by implicitly protectionist measures, specifically by measures aimed at securing a more favorable balancing of imports and exports of manufactures, industry by industry. The automotive industry has been the starting point, and some government pronouncements have indicated the intention of extending similar policies to other categories of industrial trade. Needless to say, the fundamental problem — if it is considered a problem — is the inflow of foreign capital and not the import surplus it produces; in any case, industry-by-industry balancing of international trade is an exceptionally inefficient form of bilateral balancing.

Both Coyne's monetary policy and Coyne's speeches did much to promote the causes of protectionism in Canada. But there was, and still is, considerable opposition in Canada to increases in tariffs, on two major grounds. One is the evident effect of tariffs in raising the cost of living to Canadian consumers — a subject on which Canadians are particularly sensitive because of their intimate knowledge of the prices of the same or comparable products in the United States. To this is added the political consideration that Canadian emigration to the United States is influenced by the level of real incomes in Canada relative to real incomes in the United States, the differential between standards of living in the two countries being due to an appreciable extent to the tariff. The tariff may be accepted in Canada, rightly or wrongly, as the price of Canadian independence, but that price must not be too high.

The other ground for opposition to tariff increases is the hypothesis, increasingly supported by the research of Canadian economists, that the tariff is itself responsible for the relative inefficiency of Canadian industry as compared with American, because it promotes monopolistic market organization and the inefficient use of small-scale, technologically backward techniques. This hypothesis carries the implication that the tariff impedes Canadian industrial progress and that the industrial development of the country depends on having access to a larger, international market that would permit exploitation of the economies of specialization and scale and the use of highly capital-intensive and up-to-date techniques.

It was presumably this widespread opposition to increased tariffs that led the Gordon *Report* to recommend maintenance of the status quo in commercial policy. The economic nationalists apparently faced a policy impasse. The way out of the impasse, however, was provided by Dean V. W. Bladen, of the University of Toronto, who was appointed in 1960 as Royal Commissioner on the automotive industry and charged, in effect, with the duty of finding a way to increase the protection afforded to the industry without raising its costs. His solution was a most ingenious plan, which took advantage of certain features of the preexistent system of "content protection" of the industry. Under this system, automobile manufacturers were rewarded for producing a stipulated percentage of the factory cost of their automobiles, not only by the higher price permitted by the tariff on automobiles, but by remission of the duty payable on various automobile parts used in producing completed vehicles. Under this system the cost of protection to the consumer includes not only the higher price he pays for his car, but also the reduction in the tariff revenue on imported parts collected by the government; the latter element takes the form of an unidentifiable increase in the other taxes the citizen must pay.

What Bladen proposed was to extend this system by remitting duty on *all* imported parts or cars, counting as eligible for duty remission all Canadian production whether of imported vehicles or of parts, and this whether the parts (but not the cars) were sold in the Canadian or in foreign markets. The Bladen Plan, in short, involved not only increased protection, but extension of protection of the industry in the home market into protection of domestic production in the home *or the foreign* market, through subsidies given in the form of remission of import duties on purchases of either parts or cars for use in Canadian production or consumption. In granting remission of import duties against export sales, the Plan in effect provided a concealed export subsidy.

The Bladen Plan, besides avoiding the letter of the General Agreement on Tariffs and Trade (GATT) rules against explicit export subsidies, could be passed off as both contributing to the efficiency of Canadian production by permitting economies of scale and specialization and solving the problems of the Canadian industry by means that would expand trade rather than contract it, and so could be described as "constructive" and "internationally-minded." These features were seized on first by the Conservative and then by the Liberal government, though the policy actually adopted was calculated to lose many of the advantages of the Bladen Plan while preserving its worst features. For the policy adopted remitted duties against increases in exports of automotive products over a base year and, instead of replacing the existing legislation by the Bladen Plan, simply superimposed on the existing complex and inefficient system of protection the duty remission against incremental imports. Moreover, the policy was specifically designed to induce the large American motor companies to switch their purchases of parts from American to Canadian sources, and so constituted a "beggar-my-neighbor" attack on American employment.

The fact that the Canadian automotive scheme was a concealed export subsidy scheme did not pass unnoticed by the American

automotive parts manufacturers; an action was started under
United States tariff legislation which threatened to result in the
mandatory imposition of a countervailing duty on imports of automotive parts from Canada. This threatened crisis in relations between the two countries was averted by the signing in early 1965
of a so-called free-trade agreement for the automotive industries
of the two countries. On the United States side the description is
accurate; on the Canadian side, however, free trade applies to
the subsidiaries of the big American companies, not to consumers,
and is conditional on the fulfillment of individual agreements between these subsidiaries and the Canadian government for the
expansion of their Canadian production. In effect, the Canadian
government has transferred to these companies both the tariff
revenue they previously had to pay (some fifty million dollars)
and the profits from more efficient production made possible by
the agreement, as a subsidy for the expansion of their Canadian
production of automobile and parts.

The failure of the Canadian political parties and the federal
economic civil service to formulate policy to deal effectively with
the problem of maintaining high employment and satisfactory
economic growth, and their retreat instead into economic nationalism, have had important implications both for Canadian foreign
economic policy and for the Canadian federal governmental
system.

On the international side, the trend toward economic nationalism has prevented Canada from sustaining the liberally-oriented
role in international economic affairs that was assumed in the war
and postwar years and from evolving policies appropriate to the
changes associated with the rise of the Common Market and
the United States response of the Trade Expansion Act. The
Diefenbaker government toyed with the notion of reviving the
traditional reliance on Commonwealth commercial ties as an offset to the pull of the United States, but in practice its drift toward
protectionism imposed further barriers to British trade with Canada, confined it to a purely negative and obstructive attitude toward the British application for entry to the Common Market,
and prevented it from lending its support to the Trade Expansion
Bill in the early stages when Canadian support might have secured
an act containing bargaining authority better adapted to Canada's

special interests. The present government has been similarly impeded in its foreign economic policy by economic nationalism. While Mitchell Sharp, during his tenure as Minister of Trade and Commerce, frequently affirmed the government's intention to bargain for substantial reciprocal tariff reduction in the "Kennedy Round" of GATT negotiations, the pronouncements and policies of other Cabinet members have frequently been at variance with this intention. Further, the representatives of the less developed countries assembled at the 1964 United Nations Conference on Trade and Development in Geneva were both puzzled and disappointed at the failure of the Canadian representatives to assume the role of middleman between themselves and the large advanced countries that Pearson's previous performance in international affairs had led them to expect.

On the domestic side, the failure of the federal government to devise effective policies to deal with economic stagnation has led to a widespread demand for economic planning, in the form of consultation and discussion of the economy's prospects among representatives of business, labor, and consumer interests, supported by scientific economic analysis and research. The outcome has been the establishment of an Economic Council, more or less on the lines of the British NEDC. The Council will have a difficult task to perform, since it combines the responsibilities of being conscience to and adviser of the government; and its prospects for success are dimmed by the fact that its senior economic staff have in the past espoused the ad hoc "structuralist" approach to the problems of the Canadian economy.

The failure of the federal government to devise effective policies has also given a powerful thrust to the divisive forces in the Canadian federation — forces never quiescent in the best of times. It is no accident that, just as in the United States the slackening of economic growth and the increase in unemployment rates in the late 1950's and early 1960's were accompanied by more vociferous demands for equal rights for Negroes, so in Canada the stagnation of the same period has been accompanied by increasingly vigorous demands for equal rights for French-Canadians and an upsurge of French-Canadian separatism. Nor is it an accident that most of the provinces have embarked upon economic planning on their own behalf and have asserted claims both to an increased share in federal tax revenue and to a larger voice in federal policy-making, specifically in tariff-making and monetary policy.

In any federal system, weakness at the top leads to assertiveness at the next lower level of responsibility. Some Canadians even fear (contrary to my own perhaps optimistic expectations) that Canada as a political unit may not survive until the anniversary of Confederation in 1967. I have attempted to explain how this situation has come about and particularly how preoccupation with economic nationalism has led the Canadian government into a vicious circle of inappropriate policies. If the history of recent Canadian economic policy demonstrates anything, it demonstrates the folly of indulging in the sentiments of economic nationalism — at least in an industrially advanced modern economy — and the inherent tendency of nationalism to seek to make things better by policies that actually make them worse.

7. THE POLITICAL USE OF
ECONOMIC PLANNING IN MALI

Aristide R. Zolberg

On the basis of its social, economic, and cultural characteristics, Mali should resemble Niger or Upper Volta — sleepy backwaters where, beneath the surface of a modern government, traditional authorities continue to play a vital political role and where the economy remains a minor satellite in the French orbit. Instead, mass mobilization, struggle, and planning are key words in the political and economic vocabulary of Mali, which is viewed by most observers as an outstanding example of the "revolutionary-centralizing" trend among African one-party states.[1] Since the country became independent in 1960, it has attracted attention because of the unusually austere dedication of its leadership to the spirit and the letter of a doctrine clearly inspired by Marxism-Leninism, because of the outstandingly disciplined appearance of its ruling party, and because of the ambitious nature of its economic goals.

That this militant atmosphere is unexpected in a landlocked country where Timbuktu ranks as an important town and which has been much less affected by the modernizing aspects of colonial rule than its coastal neighbors, adds to the intrinsic interest afforded by an analysis of political and economic life in one of the least developed countries of an underdeveloped continent. In keeping with the theme of the present volume, this essay will be concerned with the interaction between political and economic goals defined by the Malian rulers since they first assumed governmental responsibilities in 1957, with the strategies and tactics they have adopted to achieve their goals, and with the short-run consequences of their policies.

[1] This classification appears in James S. Coleman and Carl G. Rosberg, Jr. (eds.), *Political Parties and National Integration in Tropical Africa*, (Berkeley and Los Angeles: University of California Press, 1964), pp. 5–7. There are few works by scholars on contemporary Mali. The preceding volume also contains the most useful single essay on politics: Thomas Hodgkin and Ruth Schachter Morgenthau, "Mali," pp. 216–58. The present essay is based on field research in Mali in 1964. It was made possible by a Social Science Research Council grant in 1964, as well as by additional assistance from the University of Chicago Committee for the Comparative Study of New Nations, itself supported by the Carnegie Corporation of New York.

MALI'S ECONOMIC INHERITANCE

Although Mali ranks low on almost every contemporary economic index, the huge region encompassed by its boundaries was rich by the standards of the pre-European past. The early development of agriculture and of animal husbandry in the Upper Niger Valley provided the basis for the rise of the historic state of Mali which replaced Ghana as the dominant political unit of the Western Sudan during the thirteenth century. The attainment of a fairly complex division of labor during this period was reflected in the institutionalization of caste-like occupational groups of artisans among many of the people in the area. A general enrichment occurred after the region became the center of an extensive exchange system linking the Maghreb, through the trans-Saharan caravan trade, with the west and the south by way of the Senegal and the Niger rivers. Along these streams and in the towns that arose on their banks, such as Segou, Djenne, or Kayes, fishermen, cattlemen, and artisans produced goods to be exported by skilled Muslim traders together with the salt extracted from Saharan mines, and possibly slaves, in exchange for weapons, kola nuts, and other commodities. During the nineteenth century, several local leaders had begun to build new states, some of which were extended over large territories with the aid of traders and armed warriors in the name of Islam.[2]

These political stirrings provided a stimulus for the acceleration of French military operations launched from Senegal and later from the Ivory Coast by young officers in quest of opportunities to wipe out the shame of Sedan. Although the disappointing reports of earlier travelers had already dissipated European dreams of the fabled wealth of Timbuktu, military officials faced with the recurrent problem of justifying the cost of their expeditions reported that the Sudan probably contained huge concentrations of population which would eventually constitute a large market for French goods. This could be exploited by means of a network of railroads which would ultimately link the French Empire's Atlantic shores with the Mediterranean across the Sahara.

By the time "pacification" had been completed at the beginning

[2] For general historical background, see J. D. Fage, *An Introduction to the History of West Africa* (Cambridge: Cambridge University Press, 1959); for the ethnography of Malian peoples, see G. P. Murdock; *Africa: Its People and Their Culture History* (New York: McGraw-Hill Book Co., 1959).

H

of the twentieth century, however, it was obvious that the population density in the area was not very high; paradoxically, it also
appeared that the only precious commodity the French Sudan —
as Mali was called until 1960 — could immediately contribute to
the Empire was military manpower to fill the ranks of the famed
Tirailleurs Sénégalais. By 1939, in relation to the coastal areas
where considerable public and private efforts had been expended
to stimulate the production of major cash crops for export, the
French Sudan had become a sleepy hinterland linked with Dakar
by rail and with the Ivory Coast Railroad by means of inadequate
roads. The French encouraged peanut production, attempted to
control cattle diseases, and provided a scanty administration and
rudimentary social services.[3] The one great hope was the inland
delta of the Niger River that, if reclaimed, could constitute a huge
floodplain suitable for the cultivation of rice. With this in mind,
the Office du Niger was created in 1932 as the overhead organization for the complex scheme which would ultimately irrigate over
two million acres in the delta.[4]

After World War II, the French became much more concerned
with the economic situation of their colonies and launched planned
programs financed by vastly increased public investments. However, the French Sudan, which contained approximately one-fifth
of the total population of French West Africa, received only about
one-tenth of total public investments in the area between 1945
and 1959, a total of 27.8 billion CFA francs.[5] Since the local budget,
which amounted to only 10 to 12 per cent of the estimated gross
territorial product, was barely sufficient to meet current administrative costs, most of these public investments stemmed from a
redistribution of the common revenue of the Federation of French
West Africa and from French metropolitan agencies such as
FIDES. Private French firms never put much faith in the Sudan's
future, as indicated by the facts that there was almost no increase
in capitalization between 1947 and 1956 and that by the end of the

[3] For a brief introduction to the French Sudan under colonial rule, see
George Spitz, *Le Soudan Français* (Paris: Editions Maritimes et Coloniales,
1955).
[4] *Ibid.,* p. 90.
[5] Samir Amin, *Trois Expériences Africaines de Développement: Le Mali,
La Guinée et Le Ghana* (Paris: Presses Universitaires de France, 1965),
pp. 38–39. The CFA franc is pegged to the French franc (1 new franc = 50
CFA francs); since 1959 approximately 245 CFA francs = US $1.00.

period, it is likely that disinvestment was occurring as large commercial firms closed their Sudanese branches while others abandoned their marginal plants.[6]

By the end of the colonial era Sudan's gross national product was somewhere between two hundred million and two hundred and fifty million dollars, including the estimated value of the entire traditional sector; per capita income was between fifty dollars and sixty dollars.[7] The average rate of economic growth for 1928–59 is estimated at approximately 2.2 per cent per annum, with a slight acceleration toward the end of the period; the rate of population increase — probably underestimated — was about 1.2 per cent during the same period.[8] Most of the postwar public investment had gone into administrative overhead and was not reflected in increased production. The Office du Niger is believed to have absorbed between one-third and one-half of the total; yet by the late 1950's only about one-twentieth of the initial objective had been irrigated and was under cultivation. In spite of the huge overhead organization and the encouragement of colonization, often by coercive means, production remained stagnant. By 1958 the scheme had come to be viewed as a bottomless well and was nearing bankruptcy.[9] A cotton-growing project launched in the early 1950's successfully introduced this new crop into certain regions, but only at the cost of a constant flow of investment in return for small quantities of fiber. Peanut production, which had severely declined during World War II, returned to its 1939 level only in 1959.[10] Most of the postwar growth in the modern economy occurred in the tertiary sector, which was estimated to account for approximately 31 per cent of the domestic product at factor cost in 1959. This reflected the commercial activity of French firms, but especially the rapid development of administrative and social services.[11] The total value of exports to non-African countries

[6] Communauté Economique Européenne, *Les Répercussons de l'accession a l'indépendance de la Fédération du Mali sur ses relations avec la Communauté Economique Européenne*, Document VIII/3904/60-f (Brussels, July, 1960 [mimeographed]), p. 71.

[7] United States AID estimates for 1961, published in *Africa Report*, VIII, No. 8 (August, 1963), 32.

[8] Samir Amin, *op. cit.*, p. 69.

[9] René Dumont, *L'Afrique Noire est mal partie* (Paris: Editions du Seuil, 1962), p. 38.

[10] Samir Amin, *op. cit.*, p. 24.

[11] *Ibid.*, pp. 36–37.

(mainly peanuts, plus some cotton and hides) was estimated at 2.7 billion CFA francs in 1959; about 97 per cent went to France, where they found a protected market. Imports from non-African countries amounted to about 8.3 billion CFA francs; approximately 90 per cent came from France.[12]

The situation was very different, however, in the Africa-oriented sector of the economy. Shipments of cattle and fish to the south grew fivefold and fourfold respectively between 1945 and 1959, mainly as a result of increased demand in the Ivory Coast and Ghana; African merchants acquired modern means of transport.[13] It is estimated that this trade network produced a surplus of 4.2 billion CFA francs in 1959, thus nearly compensating for the deficit in the Sudan's trade with Europe.[14]

The economic outlook of the French officials concerned with the Sudan after World War II provides a baseline for the understanding of the contrasting outlook of their African successors. For example, in the preface he wrote for a handbook published in 1955, E. Louveau, who had recently completed a six-year term as Governor, explained that the country was so poor that from a utilitarian point of view its development might well appear doomed to failure. "Hence, it is not from this point of view that France considered the problem. Faithful to her generous tradition, she sought to win hearts rather than to earn dividends." In this spirit, he continued, "it is toward the promotion of a higher moral and material standard of living that the principal efforts of the government have been directed."[15] Beneath the obvious attempt at self-justification in the light of a questionable achievement, we can detect the significant fact that the colonial officials did not define goals and means in terms of an economic effort that would lead to a "take-off" which would ultimately raise the French Sudan to the level of industrialized countries, but rather in terms of the achievement of modest ad hoc objectives, such as a greater production of foodstuffs for internal consumption, with some surplus for exports. This would increase the flow of cash and enable the local government to raise sufficient revenue to sustain a modest

[12] Ministère du Plan et de la Coordination des Affaires Economiques et Financières, *Comptes Economiques de la République du Mali 1959* (Bamako, 1962), pp. 33–35.
[13] Samir Amin, *op. cit.*, pp. 26–28.
[14] Ministère du Plan . . . , *op. cit.* pp. 33–35.
[15] Spitz, *op. cit.*, pp. 5–7.

administration and to improve social services. Colonial officials here as elsewhere were primarily thinking about "economic improvement," much as in the political sphere they were concerned with "the maintenance of law and order." In this sense, Louveau could reasonably conclude that, measured by humane rather than by economic standards, "success is complete." [16] The same state of affairs was, of course, perceived as "gross failure" by African leaders whose ideology is founded on the very different concepts of economic development and nation-building.

As self-government neared in the late 1950's, the implications of the economic situation of the French Sudan were fairly clear. There was no obvious source of potential wealth that held the promise of a rapid economic transformation of the country; the modern sector of the economy was almost totally dominated by government and a few French import-export firms, which also handled much of the local trade; this sector was almost totally dependent on continued support from France and from the rest of French West Africa. From another point of view it was also evident that, in comparison with its neighbors, the Sudanese economy was among the least involved with the non-African world and the most involved with the intra-African economic world; and although it was one of the less developed countries of West Africa, it was uniquely self-sufficient in terms of the material needs of most of its population.[17]

EARLY ECONOMIC POLICIES OF THE
UNION SOUDANAISE

Although African participation in the making of economic policy for the French Sudan began in 1946, it remained very limited until reforms in the colonial system provided for an elected territorial executive in 1957. Having obtained 68 per cent of the votes cast in the elections held under the new system and all but six seats in the Territorial Assembly, the Union Soudanaise, one of two major political organizations which had emerged after the war, was able to form a homogeneous government. Control of the governmental apparatus in turn facilitated the creation of a politi-

[16] *Ibid.*

[17] See in particular the analysis of transaction flows in William J. Foltz, *From French West Africa to the Mali Federation* (New Haven: Yale University Press, 1965), pp. 42–48.

cal monopoly by 1959. As in other West African one-party regimes, the party and the state became almost indistinguishable from then on.[18]

The economic outlook of the Union Soudanaise leadership when it first assumed responsibility for government can be ascertained most clearly from the statements made by its Secretary-General, Modibo Keita, at the 1958 Congress. During the discussion that followed the presentation of his keynote report, he explained that it is difficult to separate "the economic, social, and cultural problem" and "the constitutional problem" because the major political issues posed by the latter "must be viewed within the framework of the economic imperatives which impose themselves on Africa and the Sudan." [19]

The "constitutional problem" at the time referred to two questions of great concern to every French West African territory, since the French had opened up the Pandora's box of colonial reform with the Loi-Cadre of 1956.[20] The first was related to the final stage of decolonization: would the outcome be full-fledged national sovereignty, perhaps within a framework similar to the one provided by the Commonwealth, or would it take the form of a partnership with France within some Eurafrican federation or confederation? The second issue was whether under any circumstances the eight territories that constituted French West Africa would retain a common government or would become separate units, perhaps loosely linked by means of special agreements and with some common services. Economic considerations played an important role in crystallizing the political choices of incumbent leaders everywhere. The Ivory Coast, which contributed heavily to the financial support of the Federation of French West Africa, wished to abolish it altogether; at the same time, since it received

[18] Electoral data are contained in an appendix to Frank Snyder, *One-Party Government in Mali* (New Haven: Yale University Press, 1965), pp. 153–56. For a fuller discussion of party and state, see Aristide R. Zolberg, *Creating Political Order: The Party-States of West Africa* (Chicago: Rand McNally, 1966).

[19] *L'Essor*, Aug. 16, 1958.

[20] For political history of this period, see especially Ruth Schachter Morgenthau, *Political Parties in French-Speaking West Africa* (Oxford: Clarendon Press, 1964), pp. 300–329; a particularly interesting study of the role of economic considerations is Elliot Berg, "The Economic Basis of Political Choice in French West Africa," *American Political Science Review*, LIV, No. 2 (June, 1960), 391–405.

a very large share of public investments in Africa and its booming economy was highly dependent upon the existence of a protected market for its coffee, the Ivory Coast argued for a Franco-African federation linking the individual territories with France. The opposite pole was represented by Guinea, which preferred both the consolidation of the Federation of French West Africa and immediate independence, but was willing to sacrifice the former goal if it interfered with the attainment of the latter.

The Sudanese leaders, associated with both the Ivory Coast and Guinea as political partners in the superterritorial Rassemblement Démocratique Africain founded in Bamako in 1946, differed from both, shunning immediate independence but preferring the consolidation of the Federation of French West Africa. Since the first of these positions contradicted the usual nationalist aspirations, the Sudanese leaders were on the defensive by the time the Congress was held. In justifying his choice, Modibo Keita reminded the delegates that they owed their status to the fact that "the masses gave us their confidence because we defended their interests at the risk of jeopardizing our own." [21] Applying this principle to the present, he demonstrated that although party officials would immediately benefit from independence by securing prestigious offices and other perquisites of sovereignty, this same independence would not only bring nothing tangible to the toiling masses, but might even worsen their lot. In a realistic review of the economic situation, he pointed out that aspirations were rising without a concomitant rise in standards of living; the economy was stagnant because of the lack of investments; the territorial government could not provide a direct remedy, given its limited means. Hence the solution was clear: "The badly tilled field requires fertilizer. Our faltering economy requires new blood; external contributions are required." But since the Sudan did not have valuable resources to serve as collateral, these contributions would flow only if the party maintained a political and social climate favorable to French and foreign investments; that meant, in the contest of 1958, voting "yes" on the referendum to establish a Franco-African community. Arguing once again that the leadership of the Union Soudanaise was under a moral obligation to reject independence on behalf of the interests of the masses, the

[21] This and following quotes are taken from Union Soudanaise, *Documents* (Bamako: 1958 [mimeographed]), pp. 19–24.

Secretary-General concluded by urging the adoption of a "realistic policy" which took into account "the economic imperatives of our country."

The issue of the Federation of French West Africa was discussed in similar terms a few months later, after the economic consequences of Guinea's decision not to join the French Community had become apparent. In October, 1958, the Union Soudanaise leaders reasserted their position on independence in the same terms as above, but added that it would have negative consequences from the point of view of African unity as well. Concerning the latter, the Political Secretary pointed out that the breakup of the Federation would be costly, since the territories were economically interdependent; the Sudan would be particularly affected if its neighbors erected barriers against the free movement of goods. Reporting on plans to create a new Federation composed of the Rassemblement Démocratique Africain-controlled territories (Ivory Coast, Upper Volta, and the Sudan), Modibo Keita added that the Sudan stood to benefit financially from a redistribution of governmental revenue within such a unit.[22] It was only in the face of the Ivory Coast's adamant resistance to this project that the Sudanese finally turned to the last possible partner — Senegal. Together they proceeded to create the Federation of Mali during the early months of 1959.

Specific programs discussed during this period were fairly modest. There was some discussion of industrialization, but this referred primarily to small-scale processing plants such as sawmills, oil presses, ginneries, repair shops, and garages, to be built mostly by private foreign investors. The nearest local equivalent of the "steel-mill complex" consisted of occasional references to a projected textile plant and to a sugar refinery for which raw materials were not yet available in sufficient quantities. The Sudanese officials recognized that the achievement of even these modest goals required an enlargement of the internal market and that this in turn could be achieved only by improving agriculture. Here is where the state and the party were scheduled to play a major role. From 1958 on, the government began to plan the multiplication of existing agricultural extension services, to orient them toward community development, and to link them to a network of consumers' and producers' cooperatives, using the party as the major source

[22] *Ibid.*, pp. 45–63.

of "dynamism." These schemes received much publicity in Africa
and in Europe, especially when, after a number of leaders visited
Israel, it was decided that all national officials would become
exemplary peasants by working on school-farms a few days each
year and members of the government were photographed hoe in
hand.[23]

At the same time it was hoped that these cooperatives, combined with state-controlled marketing boards and purchasing
agencies, would divert that share of the total product which had
hitherto been absorbed by African or Levantine intermediaries
and by large French firms to the benefit of the producers themselves. Finally, the government sought to make the economy less
dependent on these firms by seeking new markets abroad, mostly
in other Western European countries, and by encouraging the
substitution of consumer goods manufactured by African artisans
(like sandals and cloth) or locally produced basic commodities
(like salt from the Saharan mines) for European imports.

At the beginning of 1959, as Sudan joined Senegal to create a
common government for the Federation of Mali, it appeared that
the leaders of the Union Soudanaise believed that economic considerations necessarily acted as constraints upon decision-making
in the political sphere. Although their aspirations were more ambitious than those of French officials, their proposed programs reflected a fairly realistic appraisal of available resources and of the
conditions likely to insure their continued flow. They were dis-
satisfied with the powerful position of certain French firms in the
country and sought to develop countervailing power; but in no
sense could it be said that they extended this to a generalized
condemnation of the role of private capital in economic development. It could be said that the leadership self-consciously postponed some of the satisfactions afforded by nationalism in order
to secure certain economic benefits for the country at large.

Yet, a year later, a careful analyst of the Sudanese doctrine,
expressed in the country's only newspaper, concluded:

> The Union Soudanaise proclaims in so many words the su-
> premacy of the political and suggests that only imperialists,
> capitalists and their lackeys think otherwise. . . . They have
> no concept of the non-political, purely technical decision.

[23] See, for example, René Dumont, *Afrique Noire: Développement Agri-
cole* (Paris: Presses Universitaires de France, 1962), pp. 169–70.

> . . . What Soudan would want is a plan for political develop-
> ment, with the expectation that the rest would be added
> thereunto.[24]

An analysis of the circumstances surrounding this apparently
dramatic shift in outlook will therefore provide major clues for an
understanding of the tense relationship between the political and
the economic aspirations of the Malian rulers.

THE ROAD TO SOCIALISM

The most critical turning point in Sudan's political and economic
history occurred in August–September, 1960, when the Federation
of Mali exploded, after merely two months of independent existence, amidst mutual recrimination and some violence. Thus, the
economic situation changed drastically before most of the programs discussed above were made operational, and the Union
Soudanaise engaged in a complete reevaluation of its approach
to economic development. But the demise of the Federation cannot
be viewed merely as a causal factor over which the Sudanese had
no control. It was itself the result of political decisions which
demonstrate the compulsive strength of nationalism in determining the behavior of present-day African leaders.

As Foltz has suggested, the Senegalese-Sudanese conflict was
perhaps not inevitable, but by late spring, 1960, it seemed to
have reached the point of no return. The long-term advantages
each country might have derived from membership in the Federation and the development of potentially integrative processes were
outweighed by the leaders' awareness of the immediate and tangible political liabilities which stemmed from the partnership. Perhaps because of a sense of great political destiny, the Sudanese
could not tolerate their absence at the helm of the "revolutionary"
group of African nationalists led by Guinea and Ghana. As they
prepared to join them, they began to translate ideological strivings
into programs for the extension of political controls over every
sphere of life. Attempts to move the Federation of Mali in this
direction clashed with the more moderate outlook of their Senegalese counterparts. As the time to elect a common executive ap-
proached, the Senegalese feared the popularity of the Sudanese
leaders among their radical Opposition, while the Sudanese be-

[24] Foltz, pp. 212–13.

lieved that *their* Opposition might be sustained by the Senegalese. Tensions increased when it became apparent that Sudan might become merely the economic hinterland of Senegal, much like Upper Volta in relation to the Ivory Coast, while the Senegalese feared political domination by their more populous partner. Significantly, the federal partners never coordinated their activities in the one sphere they both deemed most important: economic development planning. The Senegalese chose as advisers the Catholic group headed by Father J. Lebret, oriented toward a "humanistic socialism" which stressed community development, while the Sudanese turned to members of the Charles Bettelheim group who stressed "mass mobilization" and rapid industrialization.[25]

Thus, in spite of Modibo Keita's earlier admonitions, utilitarian considerations were overshadowed by nationalist strivings. This trend was reinforced by the, to the Sudanese, humiliating circumstances of the breakup: not only were their leaders arrested in Dakar and shipped home by special train, but France lost no time in acknowledging the legality of the Senegalese decision to dissolve the Federation. To spite Senegal, Sudan cut off railroad communications, thus depriving themselves in a single blow of their most convenient access to the sea and jeopardizing a major sector of their external economy; at the same time, they did not hesitate to berate the French without heeding the costs of bad relations in terms of technical assistance, investments, and markets. But economic consequences mattered little when political pride was at stake, as symbolized by the slogan which presided over the birth of the new Republic of Mali: "Rather Death than Shame."

Almost every speech delivered in Mali during the last six years refers to "the fundamental choices" made at the Extraordinary Congress of September 22, 1960, from which the country reckons its birth. These choices refer to both political and economic orientations, which are viewed as inseparable and interdependent. Not only does the state define as one of its major goals "economic development in a Socialist direction," but the achievement of this goal is required to "turn Mali into a State worthy of modern Africa." Hence, the ultimate purpose of economic development is to define and to reinforce the identity of the state.[26] From this

[25] For a history of planning in Mali by a participant, see Samir Amin. *op. cit.*, pp. 99–129.
[26] *Congrès Extraordinaire de l'USRDA* (Bamako: 1960), pp. 42–43.

point of view, it is almost irrelevant to evaluate the wisdom of economic decisions in Mali according to an economic yardstick.

As defined in 1960, socialism referred less to development in the incremental sense than to economic reorganization. The first objective was the achievement of "immediate and vigorous economic decolonization" by "reversing commercial circuits" and creating new ones "within a Socialist plan designed in accordance with African reality." In translation, this meant that the government would expend every effort to challenge the position of French firms discussed earlier. In keeping with this purpose, the Congress also stressed the necessity of establishing effective state controls over the economy, of creating an African common market and monetary zone, and of establishing economic and commercial relations "with all the peoples of the world." They resolved also to develop physical communications, to intensify agricultural production, to stress geological exploration, and to launch new industries. These resolutions were eventually translated into a five-year plan which also contained programs designed to "develop the national conscience, train cadres, and mobilize the popular masses." [27]

Even while the plan was being elaborated in late 1960 and early 1961, the government made a number of emergency decisions which reflected its political concern and narrowed the range of future economic alternatives. Given the political decision not to use the Dakar-Niger Railroad, for example, the only immediate practicable alternative was to haul goods over poor roads down to the Ivory Coast–Upper Volta Railroad, and thence to Abidjan. Not only was this very costly, in spite of Ivory Coast cooperation in setting favorable rates, but not enough privately owned trucks were available. The problem might have been left to be solved by the numerous African entrepreneurs active in this sector, but such a solution was contrary to socialist principles. Eventually, the government was able to obtain West German guarantees for the purchase of a large fleet of Krupp trucks on long-term credit; the United States government provided dollar credits toward the purchase of fuel; and the Régie des Transports du Mali was created

[27] Ministère du Plan . . . , *Rapport sur le Plan Quinquennal*, 1961–65, (Bamako, 1961) pp. 35–36. For a detailed discussion of the plan, see Kenneth W. Grundy, "Mali, the Prospects of 'Planned Socialism,'" *in* William H. Friedland and Carl G. Rosberg, Jr. (eds.), *African Socialism* (Stanford: Stanford University Press, 1964), pp. 175–93.

to administer the entire undertaking. Since the goods exported in this way — mainly peanuts — became very expensive and difficult to sell on the world market, numerous barter agreements were negotiated with Communist countries. The government then gave a monopoly over all exports of this type to a new state organization, which was also given exclusive rights to import certain categories of consumer goods that corresponded to the counterparts in the barter agreements, thus avoiding competition between them and equivalent goods imported from Western Europe and insuring the profitability of the entire operation. The establishment of relations "with all the peoples of the world" required a vast increase in official travel, especially to Communist countries. But how could Malian officials reach their destinations rapidly without using the Dakar-Niger Railroad or relying on French airlines, which, they feared, were subject to French official pressures and directives? The solution was to create their own international airline. When the French company that owned and operated an existing domestic airline refused to participate in a proposed mixed-capital enterprise, the Malians decided to go it alone. Soviet loans to purchase Soviet planes were readily available; Eastern Europeans were recruited at high salaries to provide the crews; and the new state-owned Air Mali then absorbed the more profitable domestic airline.

Immediate political survival, as well as the establishment of political controls over the entire economy and programs based on mobilization, required a reliable governmental bureaucracy and a highly disciplined party. Although the Union Soudanaise had a formidable reputation, a great deal remained to be done. Participation in the 1959 elections was so low that, although the Union Soudanaise obtained 76 per cent of the votes cast and every seat in the National Assembly, its tangible followers amounted to only about one-fourth of the adult population. Around 1958 there were party branches in every major town, but except during electoral campaigns these branches had little contact with the villages, which contain 90 per cent of the population; communications between the branches and the center were intermittent. Ancillary bodies of women, youth, trade unions, and veterans had been organized, but they did little beyond participating in parades and ceremonially approving party resolutions. The leadership had launched a major organizational drive in preparation for the showdown with Senegal and redoubled its efforts after the breakup of the Federation. From 1960 on, the Union Soudanaise spun a "spider's web" which attempted to encompass every village, office, factory, and school and tightened internal communications and controls. There was a parallel expansion of the field administration inherited from the colonial era. At all levels, the party, the field administration, and specialized governmental services were eventually linked through a tiered system of cadre conferences.

Some of these trends were already firmly established by the time Mali's first plan was put into effect. Although in September, 1960, the government had asked its advisers to complete, by the end of the year, a four-year plan designed to provide economic growth at an annual rate of 11 per cent, it rapidly became evident during the following months that some of the decisions already taken in response to the emergency situation required substantial modifications of the planners' draft proposals.[28] Completion of the plan, now designed for a five-year period, was delayed until the middle of 1961; it was finally adopted by the National Assembly on August 18, 1961, in time for the first anniversary celebrations. On that occasion, the Assembly's rapporteur congratulated the government on its ability to "elaborate such a synthesis in the absence of any exact and verified documentary data, having had at its disposal nothing but fragmentary statistics established by a bureaucracy operating with antiquated concepts."[29]

The report on the plan proudly stated that the new rate of economic growth, set at 8 per cent per annum, was among the highest in the world.[30] This was to bring about a total increase in the gross national product (GNP) of 29.3 billion CFA francs (approximately 55 per cent over 1959) in return for an investment of approximately 64 billion CFA francs. Over half of this total was expected to stem from external contributions in the form of loans and gifts from foreign governments. Mali itself would contribute by restraining ordinary administrative expenditures and keeping salaries stable while doubling its fiscal intake through increased taxation and more efficient collection. Its additional contribution would consist of surpluses from the operations of

[28] Samir Amin, *op. cit.*, 101–07.
[29] Assemblée Nationale, *Procès-Verbal*, evening session, August 18, 1961 (Bamako [mimeographed]), p. 1.
[30] *Rapport* . . . , pp. 12–15.

state enterprises; deposits (postal savings, social security funds, cooperative savings) and state banking operations; and, finally, "human investments." The latter were scheduled to take the form of public works undertaken by a "Civic Service" composed of draft-age youths and voluntary contributions of labor by individuals and communities toward the construction of feeder roads, the erection of small dikes, etc. The value of human investments was set at approximately 15 per cent of total investments; they were thus scheduled to constitute about one-third of Mali's contribution to the plan.[31]

About half of the anticipated increment in GNP was allocated to private consumption, leading to an increase of only 15 per cent in per capita consumption by the end of the period. The other half was allocated to social consumption, such as schools, roads, medical facilities, and general administrative services, as well as to further investments in state enterprises. The plan was designed to keep the balance-of-payments problem within manageable limits by means of a 13.2 per cent increase in exports, while imports were to be kept down through strict controls over the purchase of consumer goods abroad and administrative austerity.

Although the plan was also concerned with social overhead and industrialization, its major thrust was directed at the achievement of a 70 per cent increase in agricultural production by the end of the five-year period. This task was entrusted in part to existing mechanisms such as the Office du Niger and the Compagnie Française pour le Développement des Textiles which had been supervising a cotton-growing scheme since 1952 and whose contract was renewed in 1961. But it was expected that the main impetus would stem from a "socialist reorganization of the rural world." This meant the transformation of the Sociétés Mutuelles de Développement Rural, state-supervised, semi-voluntary cooperatives created by the French in almost every *cercle*, into the capstone of a network of village units, the Groupements Rureaux de Production et Secours Mutuel (GRPSM). These multi-purpose units would function as producers' and consumers' cooperatives to which all adults must belong and subscribe capital shares. In addition, the GRPSM's would draw from the operations of a "collective field," which would initially supplement rather than displace existing village agricultural enterprises and function as a demonstration

[31] *Ibid.*, p. 24; see also Samir Amin, *op. cit.*, pp. 107 ff.

field, but would ultimately become "an embryo of further collectivization."[32] This cooperative structure would be linked at all levels with party units, which would provide the "dynamism" necessary for their successful operation, and with a vastly expanded and decentralized system of agricultural extension services. By the end of the period of the plan, the national Institute of Rural Economy would supervise six regional school-farms; 150 Zones d'Expansion Rurale, which would train young farmers who would be returned to their villages with modern equipment (a pair of oxen, a plow, and a cart) and the assurance of state credit; and 400 Secteurs de Base, through which monitors would maintain constant contact with the villages. Nearly one-third of the total population was scheduled to be reached in this manner by 1965–66.[33]

Within a short time it became evident that the proposed fundamental transformation of the economy required total governmental control over the currency as well as over international exchanges, which were increasingly complicated by barter arrangements. This was impossible to achieve as long as Mali maintained a common currency with its French-speaking neighbors; furthermore, it was also necessary to demonstrate dramatically the leadership's radical departure from the economic past. Hence, even while preparing to join the West African Monetary Union, which linked seven former French territories with France in May, 1962, and while negotiating with France for continued advances, Mali was having its own currency printed abroad. The creation of the Bank of the Republic of Mali with a monopoly over all exchange operations and of the Malian franc, which it began to issue, was announced on July 1, 1962. Demonstrations by African merchants against this decision confirmed the government's suspicions that private economic activity in any form is a dangerous source of potential political opposition, and they began to "eradicate the sequels of colonialism" in this sector as well.

In September of that year, shortly before the second anniversary of independence, the leaders of the Union Soudanaise were thus able to report to their Congress that the construction of socialism in Mali had been firmly begun. Their various reports, devoted not

[32] *VIe Congrès de l'Union Soudanaise* (Bamako, 1963), pp. 96–97.
[33] *Rapport . . .* , pp. 21–25.

only to the justification of decisions taken during the three preceding years but also to the elaboration of guidelines for the future,
stated that, although the objectives of Mali are those of scientific
socialism, there is no longer a standard version of the latter; hence,
a particular doctrine must be elaborated for Mali, taking local circumstances into consideration. This doctrine, contained in the
printed records of the 1962 Congress that constitute the country's
ideological bible, asserts that Mali is undeveloped because colonialism interfered with the normal course of historical development by preventing the replacement of feudalism by an
entrepreneurial bourgeoisie which, in the Marxist sense, would
have made a historic contribution to development. Hence, the
economy was controlled by foreigners who exploited it without
contributing to it and by some Malians whom these foreigners
controlled. To end this exploitation, while at the same time over-
coming the consequences of the breakup of the Federation, there
was but one solution: "To turn the State into the instrument of
our economic reorganization and to operate in such a way as
to insure an economic equilibrium, no longer as a complement
of the French economy, but as an independent economy, founded
on the exclusive interest of our country and of its working populations." [34]

At the same time, it is necessary to avoid "the aggravation of
social contradictions which appear in the course of economic
development when it occurs empirically according to the formula
of the greatest possible profit. . . ." [35] This does not mean, however, that absolute equality must be maintained, and the party
rejects naïve versions of "socialist leftism" that condemn anyone
who draws a good salary, drives a car, or owns a house. The stra-
tum of the relatively educated who man the party and the government are not a new bourgeoisie but are the historic analogue of
the proletariat; "contradictions" will necessarily occur, but they
are unlikely to be very severe, because the tenets of socialism are
consistent with both African communal traditions and Islam,
which enjoins the faithful to practice charity. [36] As President
Modibo Keita put it two years later at a press conference in Algier,
"Mali and the Malian leaders draw their inspiration for the con-

[34] *VIe Congrès* . . . , pp. 15–16, 84, 89.
[35] *Ibid.*
[36] *Le Séminaire de l'Union Soudanaise* (Bamako: 1963), pp. 74–78.

I

struction of socialism from Marxist-Leninist theory. But we do not subscribe to its materialistic philosophy, we do not subscribe to its atheism, because we are believers."[37]

SHORT-TERM ECONOMIC RESULTS

In evaluating the state of the Malian economy at the end of the first five-year plan, we are no better off than the Malian officials who elaborated the plan itself. Statistical information is so scarce and unreliable that it is almost impossible to attempt any quantitative measure of achievement. Furthermore, a meaningful discussion of the consequences of economic policies would require a comparison of the actual state of affairs with projections based on alternative economic decisions. All that can be done at this time, therefore, is to discuss general trends.

Hampered by precarious communication facilities, the Malian economy remained stagnant between 1959 and 1962 in spite of a substantial increase in capital investment. The architects of the original plan reported in 1962 that the total increase in gross domestic product at market prices during this three-year period was estimated at about 5 per cent; except for cotton, there was no increase in the production of major crops for internal consumption and export.[38] Exports grew at an annual rate of 2 per cent, against an earlier rate of 9 per cent for the 1945–59 period; imports, which had increased during the postwar period at an average annual rate of 6.6 per cent, were now growing twice as fast. The group of public enterprises concerned primarily with transport had achieved a deficit of about 1.1 billion, while others reported a profit of 1.4 billion, of which only about 0.2 billion went to the Treasury. There had been a spectacular increase in administrative expenditures of 77 per cent, of which nearly half was in the sphere of general administration, while revenue had grown by only 12 per cent. A projection of trends indicated that on this basis the total increase in administrative expenditures by the end of the period covered by the plan would be 164 per cent, instead of the 25 per cent initially projected.[39] Meanwhile, the deficit in the treasury

[37] *La Politique du Parti* (Bamako, 1964), p. 10.
[38] Unless otherwise specified, the following figures are from Samir Amin, *op. cit.*, pp. 77–98. They are expressed in Malian francs, which are officially on a par with the CFA franc.
[39] *Ibid.*, pp. 111.

had already reached 7.0 billion, and the over-all deficit in the balance of payments was estimated at about 4.6 billion.[40]

The plan was therefore modified. The revised program of investments, adopted by the National Assembly in January 1963, still contemplated an annual rate of growth of 8 per cent but estimated that 78.2 billion would be needed to achieve this result. The share to be supplied by external sources was 60 per cent of this larger total; the balance would come from increased taxation and from an estimated surplus of 3.5 billion to be produced by money-making public enterprises and reduction of 0.8 billion in the deficits of the others. Meanwhile, the further growth of administrative expenditures would be limited to 10 per cent between 1962 and 1966. It was also decided that exports would not grow by 14 per cent a year without a substantial increase in imports.[41] At the same time, negotiations were launched to mend fences with Senegal, culminating in the reopening of the rail link between Bamako and Dakar in mid-1963. Negotiations continued with France to obtain backing for the new Malian franc without jeopardizing its status as an autonomous currency.[42]

By 1965–66, the regime pointed with pride to the achievement of some of its economic objectives. Imports from France now constituted only about half of the total; SOMIEX, the state import-export organization, handled about one-third of all controlled imports and all controlled exports, which represented about 40 per cent of the country's estimated total exports.[43] The roster of state enterprises had grown longer year by year; it included garages, repair shops, metal works, a printing plant, and a number of processing plants for locally grown produce; also SOMIEX and its chain of retail shops, as well as a chain of state pharmacies and another one of bookstores. Most of these, however, did not represent an expansion of the economy, but rather a reorganization of existing activities. Many state industries were created by merely reorganizing and slightly expanding existing administrative plants or Office du Niger dependencies; state retail shops often moved in where French firms had closed their branches for lack of profitable

[40] *Ibid.*, p. 97.

[41] *Ibid.*, pp. 114–24.

[42] They have been repeatedly suspended, and were last resumed in late 1966.

[43] Chambre de Commerce, *Eléments du Bilan Economique 1963* (Bamako, 1964), pp. 37 ff.

business; a few plants were obtained by expropriating Lebanese entrepreneurs. Some of the state enterprises are genuinely new, however. Almost all of them have been built with the aid of gifts, loans, and technical assistance from Western Europe and from European or Asian Communist countries. In this manner, Mali can now display a few cotton ginneries, rice mills, oil presses, a cannery which produces tomato paste and mango preserves, a small sugar refinery, and a cigarette factory. Projects currently under construction or advanced consideration include a cement works, a textile factory, and several meat-processing plants.[44] The Sotuba Dam, first talked about in the 1920's, is finally being erected with French aid to supply electricity for the city of Bamako. The leadership also pointed out that it had stepped up the flow of social benefits: in particular, elementary school enrollments had approximately doubled since independence; new roads had been built; there were additional health stations — and generally speaking, "the administration had been brought into closer contact with the population" by promoting every *subdivision* into a *cercle* and creating below these a new administrative unit, the *arrondissement*.

But the plan as indicated above had as its major objective the development of agricultural production and productivity. Here, the Malian leaders have found little ground for rejoicing. In recent years, there have been serious shortages of grain crops available commercially for internal consumption. There has probably been an absolute decrease in the production of peanuts for export; southern markets for Malian cattle and fish are being threatened by Ivory Coast and Ghanaian efforts to become self-sufficient in relation to these commodities. The only successful crop is cotton, which in 1963–64 had increased fourfold over 1959.[45] But this result has been due much less to the transformation of agriculture than to the continued activity of the Office du Niger and of the Compagnie Française pour le Développement des Textiles in selected areas. It reveals mostly that a policy of saturation by means of supervisory personnel (whether French, Chinese, or North Vietnamese), equipment, fertilizer, and insecticides—

[44] *Europe-France-Outremer*, Special Issue No. 421 (May, 1965) pp. 153–56.

[45] *L'Essor*, January 4, 1965; *Eléments* . . . , pp. 99–102.

regardless of cost — will necessarily bring about visible improvement.[46]

Elsewhere, in spite of the reorganization of agricultural extension services, the creation of collective fields, the distribution of plows, and the expenditure of much energy by the Union Soudanaise cadres themselves, very little has happened. For example, the annual report for a major economic region for 1963–64 indicated that, although 1,300 GRPSM's had been created with a total capital of 7.4 million, with another 8 million spent by the state for rural development, production was merely "satisfactory," i.e., the producers achieved normally expected levels for the region. There was no indication that tangible transformation of rural life had occurred. Each of the GRPSM's had dutifully established a collective field, but their aggregate yield represented only 0.06 per cent of the millet and sorghum (leading crops), 0.7 per cent of the rice, 1.1 per cent of the peanuts, and 4.4 per cent of the cotton produced in the region. The report comments that the GRPSM's functioned effectively as consumer cooperatives, eager to obtain goods from state stores, but that "they did not devote to the collective fields the attention they warranted. A complete incomprehension of the role of the collective fields led several villages to work them with little care, in spite of important investments in the form of chemical fertilizer."[47] It concluded that these mediocre results have not only jeopardized the development of the cooperative spirit but have also sown doubts concerning the effectiveness of the new agricultural techniques that are being demonstrated on these fields.

Even in the absence of more accurate data, it can be seen clearly that the Malian economy is skating on increasingly thin ice. A skeptical observer might well conclude that the reorganization of Malian agriculture in a socialist direction is on the way to producing negative economic results. Yet, although the economy is not expanding, it must sustain a rapidly growing administrative overhead. Far from helping to defray costs by bringing in revenue, most of the state enterprises survive only by drawing direct or

[46] A relatively candid eport on the Office du Niger. in this respect appears in *Economie et Politique* No. 123 (Oct., 1964): 109–19; it states clearly that higher yields have been achieved only where Chinese and Vietnamese were personally involved.

[47] *Ibid.*, p. 125.

indirect subsidies from the Treasury. The vast expansion of party
activity is also subsidized by public resources; for example, the
Ministry of Information's major task is to publish a party newspaper which is not self-supporting; the permanent party staff is
composed of legislators detached to party headquarters; and most
other party activists are government employees such as clerks or
teachers who devote a large share of their working hours to party
assignments, so that additional personnel are needed to perform
governmental tasks. The government has not improved its ability
to collect taxes and to control the large traditional external trade.
Barter agreements are but a temporary insulation against the
operations of international monetary markets; balance-of-payments difficulties are greater than ever, while the availability of
credit is shrinking and the costs of servicing huge external debts
are mounting. As for the five-year plan itself, a leading member
of Mali's initial team of planners concluded in 1965 that "the gap
between the Plan and its implementation has become so great
that it is legitimate to wonder whether there really exists an effective Malian planning function." [48]

Economic experts as well as Malian politicians are beginning to
provide explanations for the plan's failure. One of the authors of
the plan, maintaining that the initial goal of an annual rate of
growth of 11 per cent was not unrealistic, asserts that it required
merely "a powerful mass movement in the countryside, a will to
mobilize the peasants in order to modernize their techniques, an
absolute priority given to productive actions." [49] Furthermore, the
plan's success demanded greater efficiency in the management of
the public sector, a major fiscal effort, administrative austerity, and
"new, revolutionary formulas" of administrative management. In
other words, the Planner blames the Politicians, and indirectly
the deficiencies of the society for which he devised his plan, without stopping to question whether a plan that did not take the
social and political setting into consideration could be called a
plan at all.

The Malian leaders are somewhat more self-critical, as President
Modibo Keita indicated when he held up the perfection of the
Chinese as a standard for the evaluation of the Malians' own inade-

[48] Samir Amin, *op. cit.*, 128.
[49] *Ibid.*, pp. 106–07.

quate performance when he returned from a tour of East Asia in 1964.[50] So far, however, there is no indication that they are willing to reexamine their economic doctrine or their programs. Agricultural failure is blamed on shortage of means, but especially on evildoers who exploit the peasants and incite them to resist change, as well as on the "irrationality" of the peasants themselves.[51] The proposed solution is therefore a tightening of the political and administrative grid system in order to promote cooperation and the elimination of "mercantilism." The search for scapegoats continues: Mali views itself as surrounded by a hostile international environment in which the obscure forces of capitalism, imperialism, and neocolonialism lie in wait and are ready to pounce at the first signs of weakness, while inside the country, economic saboteurs pursue their hellish tasks.

CONCLUSIONS

In the face of this fundamentally negative economic balance sheet, it is necessary to ask once again whether economic criteria provide an appropriate yardstick for evaluating the behavior of Malian decision-makers in the economic sphere. Although the leaders themselves justify what they have done in the name of economic development, that is not necessarily the goal to which they attribute the highest priority. If the question of goals is raised for consideration, it is possible to view their acts not merely as irrational choices from an economic point of view, but perhaps as rational from the point of view of the achievement of another goal: the building of a nation-state. In this light, the expenditure of funds on administrative expansion, on party operations, and on the symbols of sovereignty, rather than on economically productive activities, makes a great deal of sense. Even the creation of costly state enterprises can be understood as an attempt to give the new state a tangible physical existence. The economic plan, however unrealistic or irrelevant from a strictly economic point of view, thus acquires significance as a symbol of the rulers' control over the physical environment; it is not a technical document, but rather additional evidence that the state is modern and rational.[52]

[50] *L'Essor*, December 28, 1964.
[51] *Ibid.*, January 6, 1966.
[52] For a fuller discussion of economic thought in Africa from this point

122   *Aristide R. Zolberg*

Although these various activities have led to a redistribution of
national income to the benefit of the managers, bureaucrats, and
politicians — rather than to economic growth or a more equitable
internal distribution of material benefits — it is possible that only
the growth of the nation-state can provide certain psychic satisfactions, a sense of identity for self and country, that Africans,
long the pariahs of mankind, desire.

It may well be that in a country like Mali it is unlikely that *any*
economic strategy will bring about a tangible rise in the standard
of living of the population within the foreseeable future. The
leaders know, for example, that even when they behaved in a
manner calculated to inspire confidence among foreign investors,
few, if any, were attracted. Hence, the leadership may self-
consciously attempt to substitute psychic income in the form of
nationalist pride and puritanic arrogance for material benefits.
Their decision in 1960 to risk the economic consequences of the
severance of the Bamako-Dakar rail link suggests that this is not
an unlikely solution. It derives additional support from the fact
that the Malians are extremely proud of their cultural past.
They were state-builders and Muslims while their southern neighbors were forest-dwelling pagans. From this point of view, Mali is
today not only poor, but it has also suffered a considerable loss of
status in relation to the coastal countries, which benefited much
more from the presence of colonial conquerors. By the stern criteria
of international economic and social statistics, Mali is very low
on the world scale; only if a different scale of values is adopted
can the natural order of things be restored.

It is suggestive in this respect that some of the Malian leaders
readily identify with Communist China and are mesmerized by its
doctrines. Speaking of the Chinese road to socialism, Richard
Lowenthal asks whether its ideology "does not really express a
half-conscious tendency of the Chinese leaders to give up the near-
hopeless struggle for industrializing China without major foreign
aid and to seek instead to conserve their political order on the
present low economic level by glorifying its social justice and
collective discipline." He suggests further that the Chinese example provides not so much a model for quick modernization as

of view, see Aristide R. Zolberg, "The Dakar Colloquium: The Search for a
Doctrine," in Friedland and Rosberg, *op. cit.*, pp. 113–27.

a model for accepting the failure of development "and reacting by a final extrusion of the influence of Western civilization." [53]

However tempted they may be to seek such a solution, the Malian leaders lack the major requirements for its successful implementation: a body of well-trained ideological cadres who can man an organization juggernaut; a societal environment which includes a firmly established, relatively uniform high culture; and an economy in which survival itself is the fundamental problem. Recent political events in Africa remind us forcefully that most of the present regimes lack the capacity to bring about the structural changes in the political or economic sector that their policies entail; hence, they are unlikely to remain permanent features of the continent's political landscape. As Mali approaches the day of reckoning, having exhausted a variety of nostrums and palliatives which have merely temporarily masked the serious consequences of its recent economic adventures, *something* will have to give.[54]

[53] Richard Lowenthal, "Has the Revolution a Future?" *Encounter*, XXIV, No. 1 (January, 1965): 16.

[54] The most recent serious analysis of current policy trends and problems has appeared in *West Africa*, XLXI, No. 2590 (January 21, 1967), 79–81, and No. 2591 (January 28, 1967), 115–16. Something had indeed begun to give by the time this book went to press in mid-1967. Financial agreements between Mali and France were finally signed at the beginning of the year. Although details were not made public, they appeared to provide for a series of steps leading to full membership of Mali in the West African complex within the franc zone. In May, 1967, Mali announced a 50 per cent devaluation of its currency (without an increase in the salaries of government employees) and the relaxation of controls on exchanges with the franc zone. The government also indicated that state enterprises would be reorganized and possibly curtailed with an eye to financial viability and managerial efficiency. In a speech at the opening of the annual budgetary session of the National Assembly, President Modibo Keita admitted that the state had been living beyond its means and stressed that states, like men, must often bow to necessity in pursuing their objectives (*L'Essor*, June 12, 1967). The tone of his speech was remindful of the realism of 1959.

8. THE IDEOLOGY OF ECONOMIC POLICY IN THE NEW STATES

Harry G. Johnson

Any discussion of this subject necessarily demands a high degree of abstraction and involves a great deal of generalization which may not closely fit the facts about any particular new state. Each new state obviously has its own historical background in which both the general ideology and the particular policies of the colonizing nation (whether European or American) have had a formative influence on the development of its general and economic ideology. And each new state has its own particular economic structure and corresponding economic problems toward which its economic policy and ideology are necessarily oriented. Thus there are, as one might expect, substantive differences among new nations with respect to the ideology of economic policy.

There are, to begin with, wide differences in attitudes toward the issue of free enterprise versus state control of economic activity. For example, contrast the Republic of the Philippines, which has been strongly influenced by the United States ideology on economic affairs, or Malaya, which has been strongly influenced by British ideas, with Indonesia, where the colonial background was Dutch. On a lesser scale, there is a difference between Pakistan and India with respect to the question of state ownership. State ownership is insisted on strongly in Indian ideology, whereas Pakistan has been much more tolerant of free enterprise. This obviously cannot be explained by differences in colonial background, and it is difficult to explain by referring to differences in the dominant religions; rather, the explanation seems to lie in the different inheritances of the two from the British. In particular, the Indians inherited British socialism and most of the Indian civil service, whereas the Pakistanis inherited the traditions of the British army, while they did not inherit an effective civil service to develop into a centralized and centralizing elite after Partition. The shortage of talented administrators in Pakistan has influenced attitudes there toward the management of the economy. The Pakistan Industrial Development Board, for example, has started new industries with the deliberate objective of getting them into private hands quickly so as to economize on the administrative talent available.

A second area of difference concerns the importance attached to agriculture and the emphasis given to the need for land reform; these differences reflect differences in population pressure on the land and also differences in systems of land tenure which in part come from indigenous cultural origins, in part from the practices of colonial powers. There are also differences between countries depending on whether their agriculture is primarily a subsistence type of agriculture — producing, say, for local markets as well as for the people who live on the land — or whether it is an agriculture which produces predominantly for export and so is an important source of foreign exchange. Related differences concern the relative importance of plantation and peasant agriculture in export trade. The land reform problem is probably most bitter in Latin America — which can hardly be described as a collection of new states, but which in many ways manifests similar problems.

Third, there are differences in the prevailing attitudes toward foreign investment and foreign enterprises, ranging from great suspicion coupled with the desire to appropriate or confiscate foreign enterprises, at the one extreme, to positive policies of encouraging foreign enterprise, at the other. These differences obviously depend on the nature of the development problem, on the strength of the need for massive applications of capital and specialized technology, and also on the past colonial history of the country in question.

Finally, of course, there are always special factors at work in particular new states. For example, in Pakistan, a religious state, the question of the ethics of interest charges has been a perennially important issue, since Islam forbids the taking of *riba* (usury). Contractual interest payments prevail there as elsewhere, but there is a strong minority group that believes that the religious principle should be legally enforced. To do so, of course, would be fatal to national economic organization. Again, as a populous nation of continental proportions, India is prone to develop imperialist ambitions not possible for the majority of smaller new nations.

Despite these significant differences, there are substantial similarities among the ideologies of economic policy in the new states — at least, sufficiently so for it to be useful to discuss them collectively. These similarities can be traced to a number of common factors which work to a greater or lesser degree in all of these nations. This paper will discuss their contributions to the ideology of economic policy in the new states.

Three of these common influences or factors are especially significant; in fact, they overlap and influence each other to a large extent. These influences are: (1) political nationalism, which has its counterpart in economic nationalism; (2) ideas on economic development formed by the economic and intellectual history of the interwar period (especially the 1930's) that are part of a world "milieu of ideas" which has been diffused and disseminated among the new nations, providing a common body of interpretation, thought, and policy prescription, a sort of international language of economic development; and (3) the relations between the developing countries and the advanced countries, which focus on questions of development assistance and which in turn impart certain common formative influences.

POLITICAL AND ECONOMIC NATIONALISM

Almost by definition, nationalism is a driving force in the new states. It is the motivation for their formation, the key to their politics, and also, an objective of their development, in the sense that the cultivation of feelings of nationalism and of attachment to the nation is essential to the formative processes of, and a means for the integration of, the nation and the differentiation of it from other nations. Our concern here is with the implications of nationalism for the ideology of economic policy rather than with the problems of social and political integration. The essential point, looking at the matter from a psychological point of view, is that nationalism is concerned with establishing the self-respect of members of the nation in comparison with members of other nations and with creating a distinctive national identity. National identity is a very complex concept which involves both comparability of achievement with other nations and differentiation of the nation from other nations — both imitation and separation. Moreover, because there is a basic self-doubt involved in any serious concern about identity, nationalism involves hostility toward other nations and a tendency to adopt a double standard of morality with respect to them. The notion of the double standard of morality cannot be explored in detail here, but it colors every aspect of the attitudes of new nations toward the advanced countries with which they trade and from which they receive aid.

From the point of view of its effects on political and economic behavior, nationalism attaches value to having property owned by nationals and having economic functions performed by nationals. Further, nationalism attaches particular value to property and functions which are considered important to the identity and the power of the nation. In general terms, this imparts a strong tendency for economic policy to have, as a major objective, the creation of an economy similar to those of nations that are regarded as powerful, and to have that national economy controlled by nationals.

This objective has two major aspects. In the first place, where the national economy lacks productive facilities that are considered important to the power of powerful nations, national policy attempts by all available means to create such facilities. But it is not just a question of creating facilities; it is also a question of creating facilities *under national control*. This in turn tends to mean a preference for public ownership as a means of insuring control, hostility to investment by foreign enterprises, and a desire to prevent, control, or restrict and regulate such foreign investment. Both these preferences involve self-contradictions to some extent, at least from the viewpoint of the economist interested in economic efficiency. The preference for public ownership and control creates the problem of selection and utilization of managerial talent; hostility to foreign investment imposes obstacles to obtaining capital, enterprise, and technology of the best kind for developing the country's resources.

Second, where the facilities exist but are not controlled by nationals, there is a tendency to attempt to take over control of them. This may involve confiscation, nationalization, or seriously restrictive government regulations. This tendency applies not merely to productive enterprises but also to other kinds of positions of control, such as administrative jobs in the government and positions in the military services.

Nationalism, therefore, involves an ideological preference in economic policy for a number of goals. One of them, obviously, is as much self-sufficiency as is possible. Another is public ownership and public enterprise in key economic sectors and, where public ownership and public enterprise are impracticable, extensive public regulation and control of private enterprise. A third is to ensure as far as possible domestic participation in or control of the ownership of foreign enterprises and of their management. All of this involves discrimination in favor of nationals in general, but it also involves discrimination in favor of certain kinds of nationals — that is, the discrimination is not homogeneous. Discrimination is applied particularly in favor of those who are part of the government organization itself or who can be attached to and controlled by it. This may involve discrimination within the nation as well as against foreign nationals, inasmuch as the routes by which people may enter the governmental structure may be barred to significant groups within the country itself.

This discrimination involves relying on nationality rather than on economic efficiency, competence, or productive performance in the selection of personnel. This in turn involves conflicts between the avowed determination to encourage economic development and the growth of the nation and the national economy, and the effectiveness of the means used to pursue these objectives. A great many of the problems and disappointments of economic development policy in practice can only be understood in terms of the mismatching of means and stated ends — perhaps one might put the point the other way around: that the stated ends are not the real ends but a cover for the real ends, which are concerned with ownership and control rather than development per se.

The foregoing remarks relate to the general character of the influence of nationalism on the ideology of economic policy in new states. But nationalism also contributes some specific biases to that economic policy. The most important of these is the insistence on industrialization coupled with a relative neglect of agriculture and indeed a frequently deliberate exploitation of agriculture in order to finance industrialization. This is so typical that, as Peter Bauer has remarked, the difference between an advanced country and a backward country is that an advanced country overpays its farmers and a backward country underpays its farmers. (Of course, in both cases, what is involved is exploitation of the majority by a minority, since the farmers are few in advanced countries and many in underdeveloped countries.)

This objective of policy is in large part directed at achieving a "modern-looking" nation-state. To the new nations, the power of the established leading nations is evident in their industrial productiveness; it is not so apparent that their economic efficiency is also manifested in the efficiency of their agriculture, which is productive enough to enable them to be nearly self-sufficient in foodstuffs — and, in the case of the United States, to produce an agricultural export surplus — while employing only a small fraction of their populations in agriculture. In part also, the emphasis on industrialization is a consequence of the view prevalent in most cultures that agriculture is a backward way of life, and of the tendency of those engaged in it to earn disfavor by resisting the forces of national integration.

Much of the insistence on industrialization in new states is, however, connected indirectly with the role of the nation as a military unit. Industry is desired as the foundation of military power. In this respect the development of industry and science has brought a major change in the economic prerequisites of military power and success. In the past, the capacity to wage successful war depended on having a sufficient agricultural surplus to support forces in the field; while weaponry could be fabricated by rural handicraft skills (this was a potent reason why major military campaigns started in the late summer, after the harvest was assured — a custom still observed in the two major wars of this century). Now, the capacity to wage war depends on the presence of efficient industrial capacity, both to produce the weaponry and, more important, to provide a reservoir of skills capable of maintaining and operating it. It is true that international competition in the provision of armaments is reasonably efficient, so that a nation could rely on production of an agricultural surplus for the world market to finance its military needs, but this involves sufficient uncertainty and lack of control over supplies to be unattractive.

Insistence on industrialization is not only general; it also concentrates on certain specific industries regarded as of crucial importance to nationhood. The selection of these industries for special favor is motivated more by casual observation of developed countries and by a rather naïve mythology of economic history than by rational analysis of the logic of industrial organization or of comparative advantage. In the ambitious less developed countries, the establishment of a domestic steel industry is regarded as the sine qua non of economic development. In those countries that have laid the basis for modern industry, such as India and the Latin-American countries, the automotive industry has come to assume the role of demonstrator of industrial competence. Neither industry suggests itself to rational economic analysis as especially likely to speed growth through feedback and linkage effects, and both are notoriously vulnerable to fluctuations in demand and production.

The second bias in economic policy in new states attributable to nationalism is the preference for economic planning. This bias involves some complex psychological motivations. One element is imitation of what was for long believed to be the essence of the superiority of the Russians over their capitalist competitors, in a mythology cultivated by the social and economic critics of free enterprise in the capitalist countries. Another is the appeal of the promise of surpassing the performance of the leading capitalist nations and at the same time establishing moral superiority over them by adopting the policies recommended by their own social critics. Still another is the possibility of using the controls associated with planning to secure nationalist objectives otherwise difficult to implement.

A third specific bias in economic policy is indiscriminate hostility to the large international corporations. These tend to be regarded as agencies of the colonialism and imperialism of the advanced countries in which they make their headquarters and as a threat to national independence and identity; they are identified with the economic power of their parent countries. This attitude is partly justified and partly not. The large international corporations are political entities serving their own interests; but precisely for that reason, their operations are not likely to be dominated by the national interests of their country of origin — on the contrary, they frequently conflict with those interests. Paradoxically enough, it is frequently found that both the parent country and the country in which the corporations have subsidiary operations regard these operations as inimical to their respective national interests: both in England in the 1920's and in the United States in the 1960's complaints have been voiced that, by investing abroad, national corporations were depriving nationals of employment opportunities and aggravating the country's balance-of-payments problem.

PREVAILING CONCEPTS OF THE DEVELOPMENT PROBLEM

The second major common force which has shaped the ideology of economic policy in the new states is the general climate of ideas on economic development prevailing in policy-making circles, national and international, in the modern world. These ideas were formed in the interwar period and carried down into the period since World War II, during which the new nations have emerged into independence. They have three major sources in interwar experience.

One was the peace settlement after World War I, which established the equivalent of contemporary new nations in Europe as a result of the application of the principle of national self-determination and the consequent breakup of the Austro-Hungarian Empire. The main contribution of these events was to lend a strongly nationalistic tone to discussions of economic policy and development problems in these countries, discussions which, moreover, derived most of their ideas from observation of German economic policy, the reading of German writings, and the experience of academic studies in Germany by various leading participants. These ideas were disseminated in the Anglo-Saxon literature of economic development with the voluntary or enforced migration of Central European intellectuals in the 1930's, particularly to the United Kingdom but also to the United States. While fundamentally concerned with policies for developing the Balkan states on the German model, the central concepts were presented as universals and later proved equally congenial to the psychological attitudes of the new nations in their relations with the developed countries and in their conception of their development problems. Influential economists in this group include Mandelbaum, Kaldor, Rosenstein-Rodan, and Balogh. Balogh's intellectual history and writings are particularly interesting in this respect: a fairly simple conceptual framework, translating into economic language the power politics of the 1930's relationship between Hungary and Germany, is turned successively to the war and postwar relationship of the United Kingdom (and Europe in general) to the United States, then (briefly) to the rivalry between Britain and Germany in postwar Europe, and subsequently to the relationship between the less developed and the advanced countries.

This infiltration of ideas from Central Europe into the Anglo-Saxon tradition did a great deal to implant the habit of thinking in nationalist rather than cosmopolitan terms in the Western economic tradition and to establish the fictional concept of the nation as an economic entity endowed with consistent objectives and a consensus in favor of realizing them by national economic policy.

K

More concretely, this group of economists was largely responsible for the strong emphasis on the need for industrialization, and the potency of protectionist policies as means of achieving it, that constitutes the prevalent strand in the contemporary "conventional wisdom" of the theory of economic development policy. In effect, in spite of the dominance in the mainstream of economic thought of the liberal and cosmopolitan ideas of the English classical economists, the nationalist and interventionist ideas of the German economist Friedrich List have been transmitted indirectly through Germany's Central European emulators to become the dominant ideas of Anglo-Saxon economics on questions relating to the promotion of economic development in the new nations.

The second important source of contemporary ideas on the problem of economic development was a legacy of the great depression that began in 1929, coinciding with generally good harvests in the cereal-exporting countries. The depression had a catastrophic effect in reducing the money prices of primary products, which fell much farther than those of manufactured goods — and the more backward regions of the world from which the new nations have since been created depended on their earnings from exports of primary products not only to finance their purchases of manufactured goods but also to service the debts they had incurred for overhead investments designed predominantly to increase their capacity to export primary products. Underlying this adverse experience lay the fact that, in manufacturing production generally, a major element of cost — wages — is contracted in money terms and changes only slowly, so that a reduction of demand is met by unemployment rather than price reduction; whereas in primary production prices are competitively determined and contractions of demand reduce the incomes of the producers rather than the volume of output — in fact, output of agricultural products may even expand as cultivators seek to offset lower prices by a larger volume of production. Further, the inelasticity of demand for primary products in response to reductions in their prices aggravated the loss of income to producers; and the problems of the backward primary-producing regions were exacerbated by the universal resort of the advanced manufacturing countries to agricultural protectionism, designed to improve the incomes of their domestic producers and achieving this effect at the expense of producers in the primary-producing countries. The effect of these events was traumatic, in the sense that it convinced most observers concerned with development, both in the primary-producing regions and outside, that dependence on the export of primary products inevitably meant both slow and unstable economic growth, a fate from which the only escape lay in policies of deliberate industrialization. This view still has a modicum of justification, inasmuch as the advanced, industrial countries still pursue policies of agricultural protectionism, in forms which concentrate the burden of adjustment to world market disturbance on producers in the less developed countries, and have in fact been intensifying these policies in the postwar period. But basically it is a view founded on a particularly disastrous historical experience which is extremely unlikely to be repeated.

The third source of contemporary ideas on the development problem was changes in intellectual perspective which occurred in Europe during the depression years of the 1930's in response to the depression and contemporary interpretations of it. Two in particular were important: the rise of political socialism, and the Keynesian revolution in economics.

One relevant aspect of the socialist thinking of the time was its emphasis on the apparent success of Communist five-year planning in Russia in achieving economic growth and full employment, in sharp contrast to the economic collapse and resultant misery in the capitalist countries. With this went the notion that the success of Russian planning lay in its concentration on investment in heavy industry rather than the production of consumer goods. (In the light of hindsight, this concentration appears to have been the result of Stalin's nationalism and of doubtful economic benefit; and planning oriented toward heavy industry appears to score its success by avoiding the difficult allocation problems entailed in securing for consumers a rising standard of living in an environment of free choice among abundant quantities and varieties of goods.) The contrast between capitalist reality and a largely mythological Russian alternative did much to implant among the intellectuals a belief in the necessity and efficacy of centralized planning centered on the accelerated growth of heavy industry. On the other hand, among non-Communist or Fabian socialists, the drastic breakdown of capitalism fostered the view that all that barred the achievement of the just and equitably prosperous so-

ciety was the inherent defectiveness of the capitalist system itself—that all that was required to achieve enough output to
provide plenty for all was the introduction of intelligent socialist
management of the economy, to be implemented by widespread
nationalization of industry and the adoption of sweeping policies
of income redistribution. Nationalization appeared to be all that
was required to liberate productive potentialities from the chains
of capitalism; once this had been accomplished, distribution rather
than production appeared as the pressing problem of socio-eco-
nomic policy. The socialist emphasis of the 1930's on centralized
economic planning, nationalization of industry, and redistribution-
of-income policies, to the neglect of policies of promoting economic efficiency, has continued to exercise a strong influence on
contemporary ideas on the priorities of policy in the new nations.

The Keynesian revolution in economics—which in the minds
of many of Keynes' followers, though not of Keynes himself, was
inextricably intertwined with the socialist ideas just described—
conveyed the same general message: that the failure of the system
to perform satisfactorily was due to mismanagement, and could
be remedied by the application of scientific intelligence. Keynes
himself, who was a liberal, looked to the intelligent use of general
fiscal and monetary policies to provide the remedy; his more socialist followers looked rather to planning, income-redistribution
policies, and social ownership or control of industry. But both
assumed implicitly that production and economic growth would
look after themselves if only the system were properly managed.

Subsequent thinking on the development problem was not only
influenced in a general way by these fundamental presuppositions
of the Keynesian system of thought, but was influenced in detail
by Keynes' implicit assumptions about the structure of the economy about which he was theorizing and by the short-run nature
of his analysis. Specifically, Keynes was essentially theorizing
about an advanced economy in which both modern machinery
and the skilled labor required to man it were present in adequate
supply but were idled by a deficiency of aggregate demand for
output. In this situation, attention naturally focused on the existence and plight of the unemployed labor, and the appropriate
policy prescription was to raise aggregate demand sufficiently to
draw this labor back into employment in manning the capital
equipment it was trained to operate. The theory indicated that

this could be accomplished by using expansionary fiscal and monetary policy to stimulate investment in new capital equipment, and thus through the investment-consumption multiplier relationship to stimulate consumption expenditure as well. In the short-run context of the theory, however, investment was regarded simply as a kind of demand for final output that did not simultaneously satisfy consumption, not as a means of providing additional productive capacity for the economy as a whole.

From this conceptual apparatus for analyzing the short-run employment problem in an advanced economy, contemporary development theory carried over two key concepts that have proved in the light of experience to have relatively little empirical foundation and to be dangerously misleading guides to development policy. First, the assumption of the existence of mass unemployment or "disguised unemployment" (employment in lower-grade jobs than those for which the workers were qualified) of skilled workers, valid for recession conditions in a capitalist economy, was accepted as valid for the normal condition of the less developed economies, which were assumed to be characterized by armies of disguised unemployment concealed in the subsistence agricultural sector of the economy. This assumption distracted attention from the problem of training the labor force in modern industrial skills that is an essential part of the process of initiating self-sustaining economic development. Second, Keynesian theory threw major emphasis on the level of fixed capital investment as the determinant of the level of income and employment; while this was a short-run theory, it was easily converted (by Harrod and Domar) into a long-run growth theory by introducing the effect of investment on the stock of capital. The resulting growth model, which made the rate of growth depend on the proportion of income saved and the incremental effect of investment on productive capacity, became the basic conceptual framework for development theory and policy. The consequence was to emphasize the strategic role of fixed capital investment in development, again to the neglect of the importance of the accumulation of labor skills and also of managerial and marketing skills. This emphasis was reinforced by what was believed to be the source of strength of Russian economic planning: its concentration on investment in heavy industry.

The fundamental theme of this set of ideas about the development problem that emerged from the experience of the 1930's and its intellectual interpretation was that the defects of the capitalist system were the root cause of economic backwardness, not the backwardness of people and their cultures in relation to the requirements of modern industrial society. Development, it was believed, was readily accessible to any country if it would only throw off the shackles of the private enterprise system, adopt economic planning, accumulate capital, and invest it to industrialize itself and eliminate its dependence on primary production. These ideas began to be propagated and applied with the emergence of the new nations in the late 1940's and 1950's; they were reinforced by the presentation by various imaginative scholars of theories of development (partaking of the character of myths) that either supported or could be interpreted as supporting the notion that a self-sustaining growth process could be initiated by a brief sharp national effort. These theories included Rostow's "take-off" hypothesis, according to which, once the preconditions for growth have been established, the transition to a self-generating growth process occurs in a historically brief take-off phase; Myrdal's notion of "circular cumulative causation," according to which growth once initiated feeds on itself; and the theory of Leibenstein and other writers concerned with population pressure as an obstacle to development that a "critical minimum effort" would be both necessary and sufficient to overcome the demographic barrier to growth of income per head.

This set of ideas is evidently congenial to political and economic nationalism. It makes backwardness and stagnation the consequence of the capitalist system as practiced by the advanced countries, and development a condition that can be achieved without fundamental social and economic change, and in a relatively short period of time. Further, it makes it appear possible for development to be achieved along with the implementation of social, cultural, and equalitarian restrictions on the freedom of competition and the practice of widespread intervention in the processes and consequences of industrialization. It suggests that one can have one's cake and eat it too — that there exists some mysterious source of untapped economic energy, which, if liberated, can provide both for development and for the liberal fulfillment of other social goals.

Needless to say, these appearances are grossly misleading. The transformation of a traditional agricultural society into a modern industrial society necessitates fundamental changes in cultural values and social structure, involving the depersonalization of economic relationships, the inculcation of a general concern for efficiency, and the willingness to accept and indeed strive for change. The results of trying to achieve economic development without basic social and cultural changes and consistently with the maintenance of pre-industrial social and cultural objectives were, inevitably, widespread economic waste and a general tendency for development programs to produce disappointing results and in particular to fail to establish the hoped-for self-sustaining process of growth at an adequate rate. This experience has gradually been changing contemporary notions about the development problem, toward increased emphasis on programs for the training and education of the labor force as compared with material investment programs, recognition of the virtues of competition as contrasted with centralized administration in countries short of administrative talent, and interest in production of specialized industrial products for the world market as compared with self-sufficient industrialization. But the prevailing concepts of development theory are still basically protectionist, autarkist, and centralist. In particular, the new interest in expansion of international trade as a means of promoting development, manifested at the 1964 United Nations Conference on Trade and Development, represents an attempt to extend protectionist philosophy and methods beyond the limitations of the domestic market of the nation-state rather than a conversion of development theorists and policy-makers to a more free-trading philosophy.

POLICIES AND ATTITUDES OF THE ADVANCED COUNTRIES TOWARD THE NEW NATIONS

The policies and attitudes of the advanced countries toward the new nations became an important formative influence on the latter in consequence of the cold war and its results in inducing the advanced countries to provide development assistance on a growing scale to the new nations as a means of strengthening the independence or enlisting the support of these nations. This influence has tended to support and reinforce the ideology of economic policy resulting from the two sets of forces previously discussed. The developed countries have formed certain ideas as to what a new nation should aim at and how it should behave, and the new nations, as a means of securing the benefits associated with the favor of the advanced countries, have tended to cast themselves in the expected mold.

In the first place, at least until recently, the advanced countries have placed considerable emphasis on autarky and on the pursuit of autarkic policies. The most important of the advanced countries concerned have been, as a result both of economic geography and of economic policy, themselves autarkic and have envisaged the problems and the desirable policies of the less developed new states in the same terms. The United States and Russia are by nature continental economies and naturally virtually self-sufficient, apart from any additional tendency in this direction imparted by economic policies of protectionism and autarky. While France and England are more heavily committed to international trade by geography, their policies and, above all, their ideals of proper economic policy, stress the objective of self-sufficiency as a result of their recent historical experiences.

The bent of the aid-giving countries toward expecting autarkic policies on the part of the new, less developed nations was strongly reinforced by the fact that, at least in the early stages of the evolution of development assistance policy, India was the new nation that commanded the most attention. Like the two largest of the advanced countries, India is a continental economy, naturally equipped for self-sufficient economic development. Moreover, many experts in the field of development economics have derived their main experience of development problems from a brief field trip to India at governmental expense and automatically think of India as the type-case of underdevelopment. This habit is also ingrained in the Indian economists themselves, who typically arrive at international conferences armed with papers that begin and are loaded with the phrase "an underdeveloped country like India" (it is next to impossible to find another underdeveloped country like India, unless one considers mainland China, and the pairing of the two is for political reasons unlikely to occur even to the most unworldly of social scientists). In short, India, the one new country about which it is possible to think in American or Russian terms, happens to have been the first of such countries to attract a major development assistance effort from the advanced

countries, and the basis on which they formulated their views of
the development problem.

Finally, in this connection, for obvious psychological and political reasons, the officials of the advanced countries responsible for
dealing with the less developed countries tend to think in terms
of planning within a national framework. Government inevitably
thinks in terms of national units and also in terms of planning,
regardless of whether the country it governs is nominally free
enterprise, socialist, or Communist; and, confronted with the obligation to do something about the problems of another country,
it automatically conceives these problems in the same terms. It is
one of the paradoxes of contemporary history that, in spite of the
mythology of United States adherence to free enterprise and ab-
horrence of socialist planning, United States government officials
have probably done as much as indigenous political processes to
implant the concepts of economic planning in foreign countries —
first through the Marshall Plan and then through the Foreign Aid
Program. In this activity they have been supported by the development of the basic technology of organizing economic information,
national income accounts, and input-output tables — tools whose
usefulness lies mainly in providing the prerequisites of economic
planning.

This consideration introduces a second aspect of the influence
of the advanced countries on the new nations: the emphasis of
the former on the need for economic planning by the latter. This
emphasis is associated with the autarkic approach of the advanced
to the problems of the less developed countries; more important,
it is associated with the notion that aid should be proportioned
to the development efforts put forth by the less developed countries on their own behalf. The most readily understandable and
evaluable measure of the seriousness of development purpose of
a less developed country is its national development plan; without
the existence of such a plan, carefully designed to be properly
ambitious, a developed aid-giving country cannot be sure either
that its aid is deserved and merited, or that it will serve the desired
catalytic function in promoting economic development. (The
practice of working up ambitious development plans dependent
on vast sums of foreign aid for their success, and then using these
plans as an argument to the developed countries for them to pro-

vide the required aid, is sometimes referred to as the Indian rope trick, because it is an effective means by which the Indian planners rope the developed countries into providing external assistance for Indian economic development.) Consequently, new nations desirous of aid are under strong pressure to practice economic planning — as a means of extracting economic aid, if nothing else. These observations apply with particular force to bilateral aid; but the international institutions concerned with channeling multilateral development funds are equally insistent on the presentation of national development plans to validate claims on the limited total of funds they have at their disposal.

A third aspect of the influence of the attitudes of the developed countries on those of the less developed concerns the question of industrialization versus agricultural development. It is natural for the representatives of the advanced countries, especially the United States and Russia, to consider industrial capability as the measure of national competence; industry is the field of economic activity in which these two countries compete and in which the other advanced countries seek to emulate them. Furthermore, the emphasis on industrial as against agricultural development is consistent with certain ideological or empirical characteristics of the two protagonists in the world power struggle. Marxist theory has consistently underemphasized the role of improvements in agriculture in the process of increasing productivity and income per head, so that the Russian model of economic development is almost entirely concerned with investment in industrial production. The United States, on the other hand, has been only too successful in increasing agricultural productivity, and as a result has been burdened by the production of surpluses of agricultural products — surpluses which it has been convenient to dispose of under the guise of helping to feed the poor countries of the world. This has implicitly meant favoring the industrialization of regions of the world that would absorb United States agricultural surpluses, rather than encouraging these regions to render themselves independent of United States surplus disposal policies by developing their own production of agricultural products. Finally, the discrimination of developed countries in favor of industrial rather than agricultural development of the less developed countries has been fostered by the general bias of urban-reared governmental personnel against the rural style of life and by the fact that (except

for large irrigation projects) agricultural development does not
permit the erection of large visible living monuments to the efficacy of governmental development assistance, whereas new fac-
tories or industries provide an unlimited opportunity for this kind
of monument building.

The only major area of development policy that offers scope for
a major conflict of interest between the developed aid-giving
countries and the aid-receiving new nations concerns the role of
the large international corporations in economic development;
and this is a source of conflict only between the private enterprise
aid-givers and the new nations. Even in this context, the potentialities of conflict are weakened by the consequences of the intellectual developments of the 1930's, which generated widespread
public distrust in the capitalist countries of the economic power
of big business, a distrust particularly ingrained in those who
chose to become public servants. Thus, though the conflict may
be severe at the level of expressed national ideologies, it has been
far less so at the operating level of relations between the officials
of the developed and of the less developed countries, since the
former officials tend to share the hostility to the international corporations evidenced by the latter, though for economic and social
rather than nationalistic reasons.

SUMMARY

This paper has been concerned with three of the main sources
of the prevailing ideology of economic policy in new states: their
own political and economic nationalism; the heritage of ideas from
the interwar period concerning the nature of the development
problem; and the influence of the advanced countries as advisers
and sources of foreign aid. These three sources converge in establishing certain major elements of the ideology of economic policy
in the new nations. In particular, they interweave in support of:
policies of economic autarky; concentration on industrialization
at the expense of agricultural development; a preference for economic planning and for public control of industry; and hostility
to operations in the country by large foreign enterprises.